yard full of sun

yard full of sun

*The Story of a
Gardener's Obsession
That Got a Little
Out of Hand*

scott calhoun

RIO NUEVO PUBLISHERS
TUCSON, ARIZONA

RIO NUEVO PUBLISHERS®

P.O. Box 5250, Tucson, Arizona 85703-0250

(520) 623-9558, www.rionuevo.com

Photography © as follows:
Scott and Deirdre Calhoun: pages 4–5, 6–7, 14, 25, 28, 29,
30, 40, 44, 48, 57, 62, 65, 72, 76, 78, 87, 88, 91, 94, 96,
111, 112, 115, 119, 121, 122, 124, 126, 127, 146, 152.
All other photos © W. Ross Humphreys.

Design: Karen Schober, Seattle, Washington

Shown on the first seven pages: Parry's penstemon (pages
2–3); ocotillo fence and potted torch cactus (pages 4–5); brittlebush (pages 6–7).

Library of Congress Cataloging-in-Publication Data

Calhoun, Scott.
  Yard full of sun : the story of a gardener's obsession that got
a little out of hand / Scott Calhoun.
      p. cm.
  Includes bibliographical references and index.
  ISBN 1-887896-66-X (pbk.)
  1. Calhoun, Scott--Homes and haunts--Arizona--Tucson. 2.
Gardeners--Arizona--Tucson--Anecdotes. 3. Gardening--
Arizona--Tucson--Anecdotes. I. Title.

SB455.C298 2005
635'.09791'776--dc22

2004019123

Printed in Korea

10 9 8 7 6 5 4 3 2 1

For Deirdre and Zoë,
who traveled with me down the dusty
desert path that became this book

It will be personal,
and it will be fascinating, because there
is no such thing as dullness when the
gardener is going full steam ahead
and damn the torpedoes…

—HENRY MITCHELL,
The Essential Earthman

contents

preface

"Garden" might be too fine a word for the ragtag assemblage of native plants, rock, cactus, rusty iron, and Mexican pop bottles that make up our home landscape. Our little adobe house and yard sit in the shadow of the Rincon Mountains on the eastern fringe of Tucson, Arizona. You could call our dusty garden a corral of plants, or a nurseryman's obsession run wild, but mostly our yard is a response to a powerful sun moving across a big sky.

Here in the West, you can't get away from the big sky and full light. Even as our nation is built into a coast-to-coast strip mall, differences in light make the West unique. As Larry McMurtry says in his book *Roads,* "Eastern light is never as strong and full as Western light; a thousand McDonald's will not make Boston feel like Tucson."

Except for the fact that most Americans think of a yard as lawn—something *our* yard lacks entirely—the word *yard* seems to describe what we've made. There is really no fooling around with the word *yard*—it's a straightforward one-syllable word. You've got your front yard, your back yard, and your side yards. It fits the casual, pared-down spirit of the Western American landscape. Although it's not particularly evocative, at least it is not pretentious. Unlike the word *garden, yard* is an egalitarian word; it doesn't allude to, or compare itself with, a regal European estate. Here in the

Southwest, we've spent enough time being embarrassed that our yards don't look like the grounds of the palace at Versailles.

It's high time we stop stirring up dust with our lawn mowers and start celebrating our native plant resources, which are unique in all the world. Twenty years ago, you would have been hard-pressed to find most of the plants mentioned in this book at any Southwest nursery; today, these plants, while still not ubiquitous, are commonly grown and, with a little searching, can be had by any determined gardener. In the desert gardening subculture—a world filled with horticulturists, cactus rustlers, and crackpots—finding the plants is half the fun.

So here is the story of our adventure—a tale chronicling the pursuit of a visionary landscape. It is a hot pursuit, akin to a coyote chasing a jackrabbit. Sometimes, the coyote is blinded by dust and loses the rabbit; occasionally, he sinks his teeth right into the warm underbelly. Like the coyote, the gardener is a gregarious and familial animal, and our story takes place in a family setting. It is the story of one young family's struggle to build an uncommon home and yard in the modern American Southwest—a family standing outside in a brand new back yard of beaten dirt and considering how to proceed. It is a good question: What to do with a yard full of sun?

—SCOTT CALHOUN

Parry's penstemon and brittlebush.

building the sonoran bungalow

building the sonoran bungalow—a construction document

A fourth-generation Arizonan,
I moved back here for the desert. The smell of creosote bush
after rain, the columnar saguaro, the lime-green
palo verde tree—this is my landscape.

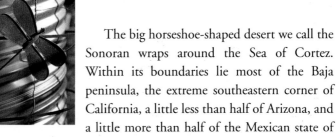

I felt the great tug of Phoenix, with its world-class museums, shopping malls, and cathedral-like freeways, but settled in Arizona's smaller and less affluent second city, Tucson. Tucson's most famous museum, the Arizona-Sonora Desert Museum, was not dedicated to artists or scientists but rather to the beauty of desert plants and animals. Where Phoenix had largely rejected the Sonoran Desert, Tucson embraced it. Mark Dimmitt, director of natural history at the Arizona-Sonora Desert Museum, puts it this way: "Tucson is one of the few cities in the country that doesn't value grass yards; [but] it is the Center of the Universe with cactus. They are enormously popular here."

The big horseshoe-shaped desert we call the Sonoran wraps around the Sea of Cortez. Within its boundaries lie most of the Baja peninsula, the extreme southeastern corner of California, a little less than half of Arizona, and a little more than half of the Mexican state of Sonora. As deserts go, the Sonoran is relatively lush and wooded. In an average Tucson winter we can expect up to six inches of gentle rain to drizzle in from Pacific storms that move in from California. The other portion of our yearly ten to fourteen inches of rain comes in the form of ferocious monsoon thunder-

Mexican fencepost cactus (opposite); Baja "punk rock hairdo" barrel cactus (pages 10–11).

storms that rumble northward from Mexico beginning around the end of June. And there is nothing quite like the violence of a summer storm for entertainment that borders on sheer terror.

This even division of our summer and winter rains, along with mild winters, distinguishes the Sonoran from other North American deserts; it makes this an arboreal desert full of ironwood, acacia, mesquite, and palo verde trees. More than just a geological curiosity of sand and rock, the Sonoran Desert is home to a remarkable variety of plant and animal forms. The candelabra-like ocotillo and the intricately beaded Gila monster are cases in point.

The relatively mild winters have created the perfect conditions for species like the saguaro and ironwood as well as the silver-haired, Buick-driving winter visitor from Des Moines—an increasingly common species in these parts, especially near golf course habitat. When you get right down to it, our warm winter temperatures have caused a lot of trouble in the desert. Not only have we deprived the entire province of Manitoba of its over-sixty population from November through April, we have created a myth that tropical plants like queen palms will thrive here. People forget that while our winter temperatures are mostly mild, it does get cold

Our Civano house under construction.

here. The record low in Tucson is 16 degrees—a mortal temperature for her majesty's palm.

A neighbor of ours, a northern transplant, once commented, "I don't think people were meant to live here." At the time, I wrote off her remark as the misgiving of a non-desert rat. Now though, as I drive around Tucson and see a ridge top disfigured by terraced lots, a new development with exotic trees in every yard, and wildcat manufactured homes cluttering up the desert fringes of our city, I've formulated my own theory: "People are not meant to live here like this." I hate to use this overworked word, but we need a new *paradigm* to develop by. As Frank Lloyd Wright wrote in a letter to *Arizona Highways* magazine in May 1940, we need an architecture that reflects the desert's own patterns. Wright felt that nothing would be as valuable as the cactus forests that tourists traveled hundreds of miles to see and that we should vigilantly protect our deserts from the greed of shifty developers.

We do have some good architectural models. Tucson's old barrios are full of simple adobe row houses that looked distinctly Sonoran, along with a bevy of tasteful desert bungalows built in the 1920s, 30s, and 40s. In addition, a few new developments introduced regional architectural styles that combine the looks of old Tucson with contemporary minimalist design. Even a few old warehouses are being converted into tasteful desert lofts. Most importantly, Tucsonans have begun landscaping with desert plants and have just about the lowest water use per capita of any medium-sized city in the Southwest.

Into this milieu of Sonoran weather, crazed development, desert plants, and historic barrios, we came looking for a place to live. My wife, Deirdre, and I were young and idealistic; we wanted to find a community in the Sonoran Desert that balanced human needs with resource conservation. In 1998, we read an

Internet story about a new development called Civano, and we moved to Tucson to be a part of it.

We learned that the development attempts to marry sustainable design with Traditional Neighborhood Development. This means solar panels and front porches, tree-lined paths and low-e (low energy use) windows, narrow streets and reclaimed water, and a Neo-Pueblo-style neighborhood center. Civano is designed for people first, cars second. For our family, Civano presented an eminently attractive choice.

We visited the site and found it stocked with salvaged plant life. Hedgehog cacti were corralled behind a fence like an army of porcupines. Rows and rows of old palo verde and mesquite trees stood in six-foot-high boxes awaiting replanting. For many months before we moved in we would drive out to the Civano site to walk in the orchard of boxed trees in the evenings.

Since the Civano development was still only dusty acreage when we first arrived in Tucson, we rented a mid-town apartment while we designed and built our home. Our then-six-year-old daughter, Zoë, thought apartment life was a plus. The unit itself was modest, but it did have a heated pool, which to a couple of Utah girls like Deirdre and Zoë was equivalent to resort living. The pool helped ease the girls' transition to Arizona life. Zoë loved the pool more than anything, and on her seventh birthday she had a swimming party there with new friends. Zoë and her shivering buddies ate pizza and cake on the pool deck in the cool March twilight.

Our tiny apartment balcony became the genesis of our Tucson yard. Using a big Rubbermaid plastic container, Zoë helped me begin a compost bin. We started several agaves from pups and potted up a purple Santa Rita prickly pear cactus pad that I collected covertly from a street median in a development called Rita Ranch. This use of the balcony was not conducive to barbecuing, and the area began to look a little like a

tiny nursery. The plants also caught the attention of the apartment manager, who sent us a nice letter reminding us that our personal items were not supposed to be visible on the balcony.

We put money down on a Civano lot, and Zoë began attending Civano's charter school. The West is full of individualists, and many of the people passionate about the Arizona wilderness seem to live on five or ten acres of unspoiled desert. In contrast, our little 6,000-square-foot lot was distinctly urban. It sounds ridiculous to talk about creating a wild landscape on an urban eighth of an acre—but that was exactly what we set out to do. In many ways our small lot was a big advantage: we could work on the yard with the sort of attention to detail that would be impossible on a larger parcel. It's not that I couldn't see the allure of living in, say, a virgin ironwood forest with only whiptail lizards for neighbors, but rather that I wanted Zoë to grow up in a place where neighbors sat out on their porches in the evenings and people knew each other's names. I also wanted to build a home with a style of architecture more organic than many of the red-tile-roof clones that were popping up all over Tucson. To me, the magic of living in the desert lay in creating a dwelling that looked at home there. It was not just about the house and not just about the untrammeled desert; we were interested in the combination of the two: the wild-urban interface. Just because we lived on land that had seen the bulldozer roll through didn't mean we were giving up on creating a pristine-looking desert garden.

I had dreamed of building a small adobe house in the Sonoran Desert for fifteen years. I read everything I could about adobe construction. On weekends, I worked side jobs laying up adobe, and I learned a lot about adobe masonry. I built adobe forts, *hornos* (ovens), and *bancos* (benches). Meanwhile, we began meeting with a young architect, Bob Lanning, to design our house.

We knew we wanted a floorplan that was square or rectangular, because this would give us the most interior square footage per square foot of exterior walls. Adobe masonry is heavy work, so limiting the square footage of the walls is important to building on a budget. Bob gave us two preliminary drawings to look at: one with a guest house on the garage, one without. Ultimately, we settled on the design with the guest house, which we intended to rent out.

Architecturally, our house is modeled after the sombrero, with a 26-gauge galvanized metal roof serving as the brim. With its adobe walls and Dutch hip roof, the home borrows from both Sonoran and Territorial styles. It also has a little bit of 1920s bungalow flavor. The design is both American and Mexican, with a touch of Far East energy.

That the house has any good energy at all is something of a fluke. Several of its prominent features stand in direct violation of feng shui principles. For example, the house is symmetrical and organized around a wide hallway (called a *zaguán* in the Southwest) that runs in a straight line from the front door to the back, right down the middle of the house. According to feng shui guidelines, all the chi (positive energy) will rush in one door and out the other. To make matters worse, we planned on scoring the concrete right down the middle of the house—like the centerline of a chi superhighway. To mitigate the problem, several experts suggested using furniture or a fountain to slow the chi down. Our architect was unconcerned about the chi problem. Bob believed

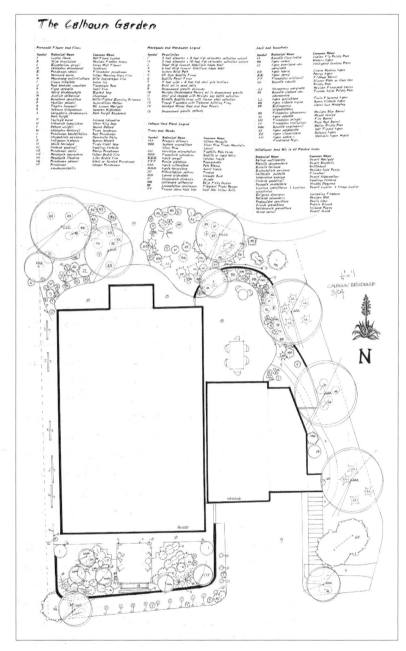

The Calhoun Garden

our zaguán was good design. To him, excess chi flow was not as serious an issue as a poorly designed roof or an ugly window pop-out. In the end, we agreed. Besides, I knew that Deirdre would find a way to make me build her a fountain in the back yard regardless. With the added benefit of using a fountain as a chi speed-bump, how could I protest?

We submitted the following design priority list to our architect and builder:

The A list: must haves

- Design and build for under $110K (excluding land)
- 1,400 square feet, with at least 2 bedrooms and 1½ baths
- 14-inch-thick adobe walls with exposed adobe interior walls
- Exterior insulation (Civano design requirement)
- Metal roof with overhangs
- Concrete floors
- Energy-efficient windows (preferably wood sash)
- At least a one-car garage (Civano design requirement)
- Vibrant exterior colors
- Garden spot
- Solar hot water heater (Civano design requirement)
- Rainwater harvesting
- Plans for guest house

The B list: would like to have

- Passive solar design
- Industrial-style spiral ductwork
- High ceilings
- Exposed rafter tails
- Circular courtyard fountain
- Gas appliances
- CAT 5 wiring

The C list: things we want but probably can't afford

- Radiant floor heating
- Built-in bookcases
- Photovoltaic system with an inverter for solar electricity generation
- Greywater system
- Screened sleeping porch
- 300 more square feet (total of 1,700 square feet)

Our goal was to build the house for under $70 a square foot. This was going to be tough, seeing that the going rate around Tucson for adobe was well over $100 per square foot.

Further complicating the project, to meet Civano's strict energy standards, we had to prove that the home would be 50 percent more energy-efficient than current new construction. Our strategy was to use thermal mass to moderate temperature extremes. The walls of the house alone have 230,000 pounds of adobe mass that can store heat and coolth (yes, this is a word). Theoretically, the home should stay between 62 and 82 degrees Fahrenheit year-round without the use of mechanical heating or cooling. But just in case, we included hydronic radiant heat, which circulates hot water through pipes embedded in the concrete floor to heat the house in winter.

For cooling, we planned on sleeping with the windows open at night to cool the mass of the walls down for the daylight hours. For the part of the year that is too hot to sleep with the windows open, we would use an ultra-efficient, water-cooled air conditioner.

Since we built the house the American way (with a bank construction loan), we needed a general contractor. We found a local green builder, David Stewart, who has an Arizona vanity plate on his Chevy truck that says ZEN, likes to cook Greek food, and listens to Jethro Tull: "It's a band, not a guy," he'd remind me.

We struck an agreement that left him supervising parts of the job and me doing a lot of the other work. This agreement, which was never clearly articulated, became defined by me doing most of the work that David did not want to do. In a strange paradox that I still haven't figured out, David was working for me but it often felt like I was working for David.

We began building in March with an informal groundbreaking ceremony. My wife, Deirdre; our then eight-year-old daughter, Zoë; Bob Lanning; Duane and Pam Bateman (our crack finish carpenter and Zoë's teacher, respectively); David Stewart; and I stood on our lot as the sun came up over the nearby Rincon Mountains. As part of the ceremony, Zoë cracked a confetti-filled egg (called a *cascarón*) over David's head as though she was christening a ship. Later in the project, I would want to crack something on David's head significantly harder than an egg.

But on that morning, with the smell of ammonia still wafting off the blueprints, it appeared that the chaos of the design and budget process was over. The plans, with their City stamp of approval, were finally done, and now the process just involved following instructions.

By the time we started laying the adobe, it was mid-May and over 100 degrees every day. The 10 × 4 × 14-inch adobe blocks weighed forty pounds each, and stocking (stacking the adobe bricks inside the building's perimeter foundation in preparation for laying the adobe) was brutal. To my amazement, with the *adoberos* I hired, we had all the adobe walls up in just over a week. The crew was a family of four brothers originally from Chihuahua, Mexico. I worked with them from 5:30 a.m. to 3:00 in the afternoon and surprised myself at how hardy I was in the heat. At the end of the job, I bought a twelve-pack of Tecate and some limes, and we sat together, one last time, under a mesquite tree drinking beer and waiting for the relative cool of the evening.

As the project continued, it became obvious that I had a better handle on many aspects of adobe construction than did our contractor. Most Friday afternoons, David would pull up in the ZEN truck and walk around the house looking at the progress. David's standard uniform was a golf shirt, Sperry Top-Sider deck shoes, and a Southwest Gas Co. hat with his ponytail trailing out the back. While I was up a ladder performing some onerous task, he would ask me various questions while sipping a Miller Lite out of one of the new wide-mouth brown plastic bottles. At one time during the building process, our last set of City-approved plans blew off the tailgate of David's ZEN truck and were lost forever.

Since I was often on the job when David was not around, I got to know many of the subcontractors. The stucco contractor called David the "drive-by general." To be fair, I should mention that David bailed me out at least a hundred times. To be fair to myself, I should say that I bailed out David at least two hundred times. But what the hell—David was excited about our project. Although he was building six or seven $500K homes at the same time he was building ours, he had disproportionate enthusiasm for our adobe bungalow, and his price couldn't be beat.

When it came time to stucco the house, we used a product made from recycled newspaper that David imported from Hermosillo, Mexico. The product is both insulation and stucco, and when it was applied to a Ford Motor Company plant in Hermosillo, it reduced its heating and cooling bills by 30 percent. After the product was sprayed on, it turned a bright white. David referred to it as the "white slop from Mexico."

The product was approved by the City for experimental use in Tucson. During a particularly stormy monsoon month, David and a two-man Mexican crew pulled up in David's truck, towing a modified stucco mixer and pump. Our house was the first real-world test for this contraption, and the job began in fits and starts. As it turned out, a large tapered, curved, stainless-steel pipe that David called the "walrus dick" was the Achilles heel (pardon the mixed metaphor) of the mixer. Several times during the application, it clogged up and had to be removed for cleaning. Once, David rushed the oceanic orifice into town for professional attention. In the end the machine was refitted with a new nozzle that did an elegant job of spewing the white pudding-like plaster onto the wall. The final touch was a velvety smooth, hand-troweled finish applied by the Mexican crew.

Just as the project was gaining momentum, we had another setback. David Stewart and D. B. Taggett—another general contractor scheduled to install our radiant heat, solar collector, and staircase—had a falling out. According to David, Taggett stole a high-profile project from him in one of Tucson's historic barrios. According to Taggett, David lost the job because he was as incompetent as "a one-eyed dog chasing a pork chop on a fishing pole." Feeling somewhat like a one-eyed dog myself, I did my best to remain neutral.

Taggett can be a bit of a prima donna who is fond of reminding you that he has "over thirty years of commercial" experience. That said, he is an impeccable craftsman. He built two state-of-the-art solar-powered homes near the University of Arizona that landed him engineering awards. His office is an immaculate garage that contains a restored fifties-era Willy's Jeep and a super-efficient Bang & Olufsen-designed Scandinavian fridge filled with all manner of domestic and Mexican beer. When Taggett looked at my plans, he spread them out on a sawhorse and lit a Lucky Strike. When I asked the cost of the water filtration system he proposed, he said, "That'll cost you two bottles of the good stuff." The good stuff, as it turned out, was Dewar's Scotch, and the recycling bin in Taggett's garage overflowed with empty quart bottles. Quarts of Dewar's became a kind of currency.

Taggett liked to tell me, "Sometime during this project I'm going to be a prick."

One morning David and Taggett were both at my job site. Taggett, who often chided David about being afraid to get dirty, noticed that David had dirt on the paunch of his golf shirt. "What happened?" Taggett asked. "Did you fall on your belly?"

After Taggett started on David's barrio job, the two were not on speaking terms. Like a child of divorced parents, I became the intermediary. The upshot of the dispute was that I would have to help Taggett erect our steel stairway and attach our solar panel.

We eased the landing and stairway into place using a 1952 Ford flatbed truck that Taggett called Peanut. Peanut had a crane attachment that we used to lift the landing into place. Taggett backed up Peanut while I steadied the pendulum-like landing and controlled the crane.

One Sunday night in September, I sat in the dark middle of my partially completed house, looking around. The moon shone through the transom windows, illuminating the scored concrete floor. My entire weekend had been spent mixing adobe mortar and filling a void around the bond beam. I hadn't spent any meaningful time with Zoë in almost a month. Our apartment—filled with toilets, ceiling fans, sinks, lights—was a place of unrest. Paying a burgeoning construction loan, along with our apartment rent, was beginning to seriously strain our budget. The bill for quarts of Dewar's was also adding up. Deirdre was barely speaking to me.

Like Taggett, I also had a habit I relished: salvage-yard shopping. My best find was some fine plywood bookshelves freshly removed from a psychiatric treatment center. Like all of my salvaged treasures, these were temporarily relocated from the Barnet and Shore salvage yard to our apartment living room—which wouldn't have been a problem if our entire living room wasn't already filled with plumbing fixtures and book-shelves. Deirdre called the big rectangular boxes my "coffins." These fixtures made using our living room impossible. Deirdre commented that the chaos was driving her crazy and that if it didn't end soon she might put me in one of my coffins. By this time in the project, I was nearly ready to oblige her. If there was one thing that sounded good, it was a long nap. I did relocate the bookshelves out on the balcony, which was the cause of the second, not-as-nice-as-the-first, letter from our apartment manager.

Although the house was nearly complete, a move-in date seemed distant. My life had become a punch list of tasks dictated by the house. I had every reason to resent this house, but I didn't. This night, sitting alone on my living room floor, surrounded by 230,000 pounds of adobe block that I had helped make and lay up, I felt a strange and profound sense of peace. The window casing that Duane Bateman and I had made while listening to the Rolling Stones was well done. The moon shadow from palo verde branches made a pattern on the floor. There in the dark, I was proud of my project—blemishes and all. For a moment, it didn't seem to matter if I ever got to live in the house. Its design and construction pleased me. Like the plans blowing off the tailgate of David's ZEN truck, what was meant to be would be. I was in the center of something I had created, surrounded by positive energy. Sitting there in the middle of the zaguán, I could almost feel the chi rushing up my back and through my hair like a wave.

We moved in, on questionable legal grounds, in the middle of November. Our apartment lease was up, and our only financial option was to move into our partially completed house. Our first night we slept on the floor in sleeping bags. First the new silence, and then the coyotes, kept us up most of the night.

There was no hot water or heat. Southwest Gas would not turn the gas on without a final inspection from the City. We had called for the final inspection, but failed on several items.

We had a leak in one of the still non-functioning water heaters. I called Taggett on my cell phone in the utility room to see if he could come out and fix it.

"Just tighten it," he said.

"Tighten what?" I asked, feeling around the water heater frantically for the loose connection.

"The supply line! Just tighten the goddamn supply line! I told you I was going to be a prick before this project was done."

Taggett had made good on his promise. This was his day of prickiness.

One morning just after we moved in, I entered the bathroom to find my wife in the tub. She was washing her hair under a cold spigot. When we went camping, Deirdre never wanted to be far from a real toilet and real showers. Always the prissiest girl in her family, the way she had worked and scrounged to build this house surprised me. And here she was roughing it in a cold tub without complaint. A deep feeling of love and respect for my wife came over me. I started to say something but she interrupted. "Don't," she said. "Don't talk to me now." It appeared that our relationship would ebb until the hot water flowed.

Without heat, the house was just a little shy of being comfortable. It was probably perfectly comfort-able to a Swede. I put a little digital thermometer on the tile countertop. The indoor temperature of the unheated house stayed remarkably consistent. Even on nights when the mercury fell below freezing outside, the indoor temperature varied only one or two degrees between the daytime and nighttime. The house was 64.7 degrees Fahrenheit in the evening and 63.4 degrees in the morning, and it would maintain this temperature range almost indefinitely. This was good and bad. It is a fine temperature for sleeping under, say, a down comforter, yet uncomfortable for sitting around in anything less than sweats.

The passive solar heating aspect of our house was a limited success. The two south-facing bedrooms are noticeably warmer than the north-facing kitchen/dining/living room. During the design phase, we were unable to optimize the solar orientation of the home because of the small size and irregular shape of our lot. Ideally, passive solar homes should sit with the long axis running east-west. In our home the long axis runs north-south. This means that we had to fudge, so we created a "solar canopy" on the second-story guest house. This canopy, or awning, is actually a solar panel for heating domestic hot water for the main and guest houses.

We had temporarily attached this solar panel to the second-story canopy frame early in the project. After one of the steel clamps securing the panel was stolen, the whole 4 × 8-foot panel blew off the frame in a severe thunderstorm. The storm must have been spectacularly violent, because when I found the panel, its twisted carcass was sitting in the middle of the street, surrounded by a glitter of tempered glass. The shards looked a little like stardust. I gave the broken panel to a guy from Phoenix who wanted to rehabilitate it to heat his pool.

With Taggett's begrudging help, I humped another solar panel up the stairs. Even considering the hassle, the prospect of hot water from the sun was delicious.

Sometime soon, I thought, our house will be finished. A high adobe wall will surround the back yard. Queen's wreath will climb the steel stairway, and Indian fig will grow under the mesquite and acacia trees. Deirdre and I will talk again in that peaceful way married people sometimes talk. The day-to-day events of our lives will descend from chaos to normalcy.

And yet, when our lives settle into this stillness, I thought, my satisfaction might be tinged with sadness.

The process of building my own house had been filled with adventure. Surely, there were compromises. Certainly, there were mistakes. But more often than not, we held on to the vision of this Sonoran bungalow with a vengeance. Standing back and looking at a three-quarter moon reflecting off my corrugated steel roof, I was almost proud.

Three days before Christmas, we passed our final inspection and got the gas turned on. We fired up our radiant floor heat and hot water heater. To get the radiant heat running, I banged on the check valves with a block of wood until the copper supply pipe got hot. As the floor warmed, we crawled all over the house on our hands and knees grinning like idiots. We all took hot showers that afternoon.

The postpartum sadness I had anticipated on completion of the house never settled in. I began a new job managing the Civano Nursery. Deirdre and I started reading gardening books together in the evening. With the house completed, the garden was our new passion. Often, we talked in the peaceful way married people sometimes do.

The finished product

- 1,580-square-foot main house, 3 bedrooms, 2 baths
- 350-square-foot guest house
- 14-inch-thick adobe walls on main house
- 26-gauge metal corrugated roof
- Designed and built for $78 per square foot
- Wood-sash low-e windows
- Solar hot water heater for household use
- Radiant floor heat
- CAT 5 wiring
- Greywater system (partially installed)
- Rainwater harvesting
- Built-in bookcases
- Exposed rafter tails
- High ceilings

north by southwest

north by southwest— a great basin yard

Envisioning our new Arizona yard
made us reminisce about building our first landscape in Utah,
which hooked us on xeric, or dry, gardening.

The early 1990s was an exciting time to be gardening in the West. Denver and Phoenix were promoting a new type of water-efficient landscaping called Xeriscape, and a few pioneering gardeners and designers were incorporating native plants into landscapes. For me, Xeriscape offered freedom from the monotony of lawn and from a lot of old, tired ideas about what a yard should look like. I studied a glossy brochure from Arizona called *Visions of Xeriscape* and dreamed of adapting the concepts to a Utah garden. My favorite garden in the pamphlet was a Carrie Nimmer-designed desert cottage garden full of wildflowers mingling with big succulent agaves and mesquite trees—a true Arizona garden. Since I couldn't be in Arizona, I wanted to make a true Utah garden.

We began building our home on a little hill full of one-seed juniper (*Juniperus monosperma*) in 1993. The surrounding terrain was classic Great Basin desert. The hills were full of big sagebrush (*Artemisia tridentata*), rabbitbrush (*Ericameria nauseosa*), and cliff rose (*Purshia mexicana*).

We picked a tough neighborhood to build a native yard in. Our neighbors were installing Kentucky bluegrass from sidewalk to foundation. Each Saturday morning, we awoke to the sputter and drone of gas-powered mowers. On a street of forty or so homes, we were one of two non-practicing Mormon (Jack Mormon) families, and we were the only family without turf in our front yard. In this part of Utah, a yard without turf stood out like a beer bottle in the recycle bin.

Throughout the 1980s and 90s, the second-driest state in the nation had the unenviable distinction of being at or near the top of the list of states with the highest water consumption per capita. In the mid 1990s, Utahans used more water than any other state, over three hundred gallons per day per person. Even in one of the most politically conservative states in the country, this didn't sit well, and the governor called for research on the issue. The experts came up with a variety of reasons why water use was so high: the fact that most Utahans live near canyons with plentiful water, the larger lot size of most Utah homes, the aridity of the climate, and even the large amount of turf planted at Utah homes. One researcher suggested that Utahans have long viewed water as a public entitlement. Although these were all contributing factors, the researchers missed the overarching point: Utahans had rejected the desert in their landscapes. In Utah, turf reigned supreme, and thrifty desert plants were largely ignored in favor of thirsty exotics.

Inside the home, Utahans used almost exactly the same amount of water as other American families. The problem was, 63 percent of the residential water used in Utah was used outdoors, most of it lavished on bluegrass.

In my view, the landscaping habits of modern suburban Utahans needed rethinking. Did every yard really need all that grass? I felt the stirrings of the pioneer spirit when I started collecting native plants for my Utah yard. To me, Brigham Young's admonition

Bigtooth maple and big sagebrush figured prominently in our Utah yard (below); golden columbine (inset); Texas betony (pages 22–23).

to make the Utah desert "bloom like a rose" was the start of the turfing of the desert. The only rose I wanted the Utah desert to bloom like was the cliff rose, a native shrub of stunning drought tolerance and rugged character. I was not going to lean back on easy old traditions—I would forge ahead into the little-known.

Using wild plants made the yard infinitely more interesting; it was the difference between a blow-dried Persian cat and a cougar. Like the cougar, native plants would fend for themselves and were suited for local conditions. On the other hand, turf and peonies, like the Persian cat, would require a level of pampering that I was unwilling to give.

Besides, plants like big sagebrush just seemed to fit in this country of jagged granite mountains and big dry sky. Big sagebrush is a generous plant with stinky silver leaves and shaggy bark. It has as much Western style as anything I've ever seen. It is tougher than Clint Eastwood and as authentic as a Lehi rodeo belt buckle.

Until I began building my Arizona yard, I thought the soil conditions at our Utah home were as bad as they came. The lot was a baking piece of compacted alkaline clay. For my birthday, my mother-in-law delivered me a truck full of composted horse manure; at the time, I was unsure of the meaning of this gesture. Using my in-laws' 1976 Toyota pickup with holes in the floorboards and dried goat spit on the dashboard, I put eight more truckloads of manure on my front yard. With a Troy-Bilt tiller, I bounced and sparked across the rocky clay until the manure was worked into the dirt. What couldn't be worked in with a tiller I worked with a pick and shovel.

The plumbing in our yard got the attention of our neighbors. After many long conversations with Mike, the Rainbird customer-support operator, I made a plan to install drip irrigation in my garden. I had worked

Giant snapdragon gives oomph to the late spring garden.

with drip systems in Arizona and knew how water-efficient they could be. Drip would also provide the deep, infrequent water that would help my natives and desert-adapted plants thrive. Drip irrigation was uncommon in Utah then, and our project had turned into a neighborhood novelty. One Saturday morning as I was installing the small drip emitters at the base of each plant, one neighbor asked, "Are those little speakers to talk to your plants?"

Our Utah garden was organized around plants of unrecognized beauty. Plants like big sagebrush and rabbitbrush were customarily bulldozed and turfed over after construction, but these were signature plants of the Great Basin desert, and I would be damned if I wasn't going to use them in my garden. My plant selection baffled most of my neighbors. A Utah native next door remarked, "I've seen a lot of people pull out rabbitbrush, but I've never seen anyone plant it."

Dierdre and I drew and re-drew our landscape plan for the front until we were both satisfied. The front yard was designed with a dry streambed running through it on a diagonal. On the hot strips adjacent to the sidewalk, we wanted rabbitbrush and Tohoka daisy (*Aster tanacetifolius*). In fall when these plants bloomed, this part of the yard would be chromatic yellow with purple accents. These varieties were ubiquitous along almost any roadside between Salt Lake and Santa Fe. Strangely enough, bringing common wild plants into the yard made our yard uncommon.

Finding wild plants for sale in northern Utah in the early nineties was another story. It was harder than buying liquor on Sunday in Provo. The nurseries near our home didn't carry and wouldn't order many of the plants on our list. We finally found one nursery that was a jewel box of plants and service: Willard Bay Gardens. Della and Barney Barnett, the proprietors there, were a husband-and-wife team of horticulturists who grew several hundred varieties of perennials in little

4½-inch pots in a tiny town north of Ogden. Della and Barney had a passion for unusual plants.

Driving up to Willard Bay became a twice-annual tradition in our family. We would often stop at Antelope Island on the way to look for birds or go mountain biking. Sparsely populated, with its own herd of buffalo in the middle of the Great Salt Lake, Antelope Island is a true desert island. I liked to think that the flora of the Salt Lake valley must have looked similar to Antelope Island's when the first Mormon settlers arrived with Brigham Young in 1847. The shoreline of the Great Salt Lake was Terry Tempest Williams country, home to the great throngs of birds she lyrically described in her book *Refuge*. In May of 1989, just before Deirdre and I were married, we attended a Terry Tempest Williams lecture. Afterward, she inscribed the following message to me in a copy of her book *Coyote's Canyon:* "Bless you in your perceptions of the desert, we need them." It's a message I've tried to take to heart.

Our arrival at Willard Bay Gardens was always exciting. Although the plain storefront resembled a 1950s motor lodge, the merchandise and service were exceptional. Thousands of flats of perennials were arranged on the benches, with neat handwritten signs. Since they were perennials, most of the plants were not in color— the opposite of the kind of retail plant whoring that Wal-Mart and Home Depot do with annuals. Willard Bay's plants were well adapted to our region, and rather than putting them in big containers to raise the prices, Barney and Della sold only tiny 4½-inch pots, because they knew the plants would do better if they started small. Barney, who on the surface appeared sedate, was really a bubbling volcano of plant passion. When he sensed the intensity of my plant insanity, he'd become animated and would want to show off some of his best work. He took us on impromptu field trips, including secret rock gardens filled with native and desert-adapted plants. We took pictures, made notes, bought hundreds

of plants, and achieved the highest discount level possible without stealing. I hold Della and Barney partly responsible for getting me into the horticulture business; they are the kind of generous and decent people who represent the best of the industry.

Unfortunately, Della and Barney grew mostly herbaceous perennials and hardly any woody shrubs or trees. We searched and searched and finally found an unlikely source for the shrubs and trees we were looking for: the Utah State Penitentiary. The State Pen had a little nursery that grew native plants to stabilize dis-

Our eclectic rock wall planting.

turbed roadsides. The plants were all in long skinny grow tubes. We bought piñon pine, rabbitbrush, big sage—all grown with the convict touch. Although they were small, the first group of plants grew well, and within a short time we were headed back to the jailhouse for more.

Because the last trees on our list (bristlecone pine, *Pinus aristata*) were glacially slow growing, we wanted to find larger specimens than they had at the prison. We finally found a wholesale nursery north of Salt Lake City that sold us the plants at wholesale prices on the condition that we wouldn't tell anyone.

My favorite part of the yard turned out to be the steep rock garden beside our porch. We built the wall to stabilize a bank beside the garage, but we left lots of little pockets to stuff full of plants. The slope was crested with yarrow and filled with low-growing rock penstemons, grasses, and bulbs. One of the penstemons (*Penstemon* 'U.S.U.', or Utah State University penstemon) was a low-growing cultivated variety that turned into a gorgeous pink mound in late spring and early summer. Barney and Della had gotten the plant from Utah State University just before the university's penstemon program was wiped out by fire blight, a deadly plant disease. I felt lucky to have it.

The rock garden was a puzzle of colorful pieces that somehow fit together. The embankment was steep but not too steep to climb. Zoë, then a toddler, would spend a whole morning scaling the rocks and picking flowers.

Like wild animals, native plants can be unpredictable in the garden. One of my wild plants, silver sage (*Artemisia ludviciana*), decided to take over the entire rock garden. It was a ruthless competitor and I had to intervene to stop it. My silver sage was proliferating faster than Walgreens drugstores, which lately seem to appear magically overnight on every vacant corner lot. I wondered about my silver sage, as I wonder about Walgreens: do we really need another one of

Purple Colorado four o'clock in full bloom at the top of the rock wall.

these here? Most of the time the answer was no, and I went around on my hands and knees and began pulling the sinuous silver roots out from under boulders. I still don't know what to do about Walgreens, but that's another story.

At the top of the rock wall, we planted a little Colorado four o'clock (*Mirabilis multiflora*) that we mail-ordered from Plants of the Southwest in Santa Fe. The plant arrived in a 2½-inch pot, but by the second year it had turned into a six-foot-wide mound of purple flowers and blue-green foliage. This tuberous night-blooming plant attracted hawk moths by the dozen. In the winter the giant mass of foliage would turn tan and cleanly snap off at the ground. Come spring, the tuber would sprout again and the plant would grow fiercely until frost.

Another chief feature in this garden was a flagstone pathway covered with thymes and lined with lavender, coral bells, and golden columbine. This pathway led to a circular flagstone seating area and was the main access route through the center of the garden. The soft thyme provided a quilt of color that felt good on bare feet and could be used to cook with (hopefully not in that order). Zoë loved to toddle back and forth across it.

This garden also included drought-adapted plants from other arid regions. As Lauren Springer, the high priestess of Rocky Mountain gardening, says in her 1994 book, *The Undaunted Garden,* "Certainly native plants can beautify a garden, especially by helping it look regionally appropriate. To think that natives can go it alone, planted out into the 'wilderness' that is an uncontrolled garden just as they do in the natural environment, is wrong."

In my Utah yard, I introduced various thyme varieties. Dwarf mugo pine and candytuft made appearances next to coral bells and rugged natives like bristlecone pine and big sagebrush. 'Homestead Purple,' a hybrid verbena, sidled up to native Apache plume. The first year, there was a lot of mulch with little plants poking through. The second year, the plants took over.

Big sagebrush, creeping thyme, lavender, and coral bells mingle along the flagstone path.

One non-native tree, the Russian olive (*Elaeagnus angustifolia*), caused a multigenerational conflict. My mother's father, Richard Graehl, had come to see our new garden. I respected my grandfather's opinion. He had been working five acres north of Salt Lake for as long as I could remember. He owned a real tractor. When I was a kid, we dreaded visiting in summer because we knew there would be a lot of weeding raspberries and mowing alfalfa and other outside chores. I secretly enjoyed these chores, and I'm proud that some of Grandpa's dirt smarts rubbed off on me. Grandpa was much more interested in edible plants than in ornamentals, and I wondered how he would react to my new garden. When he saw the Russian olive planted prominently in the front garden, all the blood drained from his face, and I saw his fists clench. "I've been digging out Russian olives for thirty years," he said. "You've got to get rid of that right away." He was dead right.

Within a few months it had sent up suckers far beyond the area I had envisioned for the tree. Although it wasn't a native plant, we had planted it for the weeping silver foliage and general toughness of the plant. I had ignored the advice of Denver-area plantsman Jim Knopf, who wrote in his 1991 book, *The Xeriscape Flower Gardener,* "These trees [Russian olives] have become a serious invasive problem in many Rocky Mountain floodplain areas. This has prompted a growing opinion that they should not be used (even occasionally) as landscape plants." Sometimes, we have to learn for ourselves. So without Deirdre's consent, I chopped down and dug up every last Russian olive root. In its place, I planted a bigtooth maple (*Acer grandidentatum*) that completed a trio along the dry streambed.

In the hottest areas with the worst soil, some aggressive plants may accomplish wonders. In just such an area, we planted Mexican evening primrose (*Oenothera speciosa*) beneath a big sagebrush. It provided a good spring show of pink flowers, and because of the dry conditions, it pretty much stayed in the general area where we planted it.

For a landscape grown by prisoners and planted by Jack Mormons, I was happy with the result. Even my most uptight neighbors complimented me on the beautiful roadside weeds in my yard. After it had grown in, the garden won an award and was featured on a few tours. From time to time passersby would knock on the door and ask to look at our plants.

The recognition was fine, but what we really liked was spending time out on the porch, watching hummingbirds and hawk moths come and go. We had created a stylized Great Basin. All in all, digging it, planting it, watering it—it made us happy. It was a true Utah yard—it belonged there like cliff rose on the hillside.

Our Utah garden trees and shrubs

- Apache plume, big sagebrush, bigtooth maple, bristlecone pine, curl-leaf mountain mahogany, dwarf mugo pine, fringed sage, piñon pine, rabbitbrush, silver sage, three leaf sumac, true mountain mahogany

Our Utah garden perennials

- blackfoot daisy, catmint, Colorado four o'clock, coral bells, double bubble mint, firewheel, giant snapdragon, golden columbine, 'Homestead Purple' verbena, licorice mint, mat penstemon, Mexican evening primrose, Missouri evening primrose, Pitcher's sage, Rocky Mountain iris, Rocky Mountain penstemon, Russian sage, scarlet penstemon, upright verbena, Utah State University penstemon, whirling butterflies

designing the sonoran garden

designing the sonoran garden— finding the big ideas

As we stood looking at our new
Sonoran bungalow surrounded by beaten earth,
we knew we wanted to bring the magical world
of the desert to that dirt.

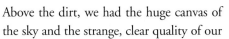

Above the dirt, we had the huge canvas of the sky and the strange, clear quality of our Western light. In *Roads,* Larry McMurtry calls the early morning light in Tucson "a river of bright air" and remarks that Tucsonans celebrate that early light as wine drinkers savor a "special bouquet." Against this impressive backdrop, anything we did in the garden would look small and insignificant; fools that we are, we charged ahead. We began by looking around, first to the Rincon Mountains to our east, and then at our new house.

It was the architectural style of the house that gave us the first clues about how to design the garden. Our house has a vibe both Anglo and Hispanic—adobe block with clean simple woodwork. I like to think that our house resembles something an enterprising Irish immigrant rancher would have built in southern Arizona at the beginning of the last century. It is informal and practical, built of local materials with civilized finish treatments.

Because of the design of the house, we suspected we would plant the garden in an informal cottage-garden style. From the work I had done on the premises already, I knew that the soil was heavy and difficult and would require plants with a special brand of resilience.

To clarify our initial impressions of what would work, we put our ideas down in a list, which didn't feel

Parry's penstemon (opposite); 'Los Angeles' torch cactus and Mexican gold poppy (pages 32–33).

like the best way to conceptualize our garden. We realized a list was too linear for a project as circular and fluid as a garden.

Next, Deirdre and I sat at the kitchen table and sketched out different versions of the front and back yards. I can't say that these were amiable discussions. Two strong-willed firstborns, we stubbornly held to our own ideas and were slow to compromise. The presence of our sweet daughter Zoë was probably the only thing that kept us from an all-out design war.

As a way of de-escalating the situation, we decided to make a "mind map." The mind map, a concept developed by English author and educator Tony Buzan, involves clustering ideas on paper rather than listing them. This is designed to use both the right and left sides of the brain.

As you can see from our drawing, our mind map is a sort of scrambled-up flow chart consisting of lines and shapes and drawings that all somehow connect with each other. It is midway between a brainstorming list and a conceptual landscape plan. It is helpful because it distracts you from thinking about the physical shape of the garden and makes you look inward at your priorities. For us, our mind map distilled the myriad options down to three big ideas:

- Celebrate Native Plants
- Save Water
- Live Outside

Around these three big ideas, many smaller ideas orbited like moons around planets.

Celebrate Native Plants

As plant people, much of our enthusiasm for this new garden revolved around the selection of native vegetation. We knew that if we were careful and a little lucky in combining native species, our garden could embody the spirit of the Arizona landscape. Although the garden would be an abstraction and enhancement of the natural landscape, its plants and patterns would recall the Sonoran Desert. To pull this off, we would have to be as cagey as urban coyotes.

Designing wildness into our garden became a high priority. We decided to let most seeds germinate where they fell. We would let our desert shrubs take on bold natural forms. We would practice minimal pruning. No formal clipped hedges, no poodled topiaries. This garden would be the cougar, not the blow-dried Persian cat.

This celebration of Western American style was liberating. No grass, no formal borders, no carefully bred annuals, no servitude to tired European design models. Our garden would be a response to a powerful sun moving across a big sky. We would defy tradition like a saguaro giving a great green middle finger to a manicured boxwood hedge.

Deirdre and I hashed out much of the design philosophy of our yard on family drives and hikes through the desert with Zoë. We would rattle off the common and botanical names such as *Simmondsia* and *Parkinsonia florida,* much to Zoë's disgust. She would look at us, in our excited plant-talking frenzy, and roll her eyes. The worst possible punishment we could dish out was a trip to a botanical garden. For a while I feared we had ruined her, that she would hate plants her entire life.

Although our garden would eschew the manicured look of some European gardens, it owed a large debt to several English gardeners. In fact, wild gardening in Britain has a longer history than most American gardeners suspect. William Robinson's 1870 book, *The Wild Garden,* rails against the overuse of exotic plants and advocates the creation of gardens with British wildflowers. Robinson's own garden at Gravetye in Sussex was one of the first to feature a naturalistic meadow planted with indigenous plants. Along with Gertrude Jekyll, Robinson is largely given credit for popularizing the most common garden style of the past century: the informal cottage garden. Even in the godforsaken desert crawling with scorpions and rattlesnakes, the idea of an informal cottage-style garden has pull. I couldn't get the idea out of my head. Could we really create a desert cottage garden?

Oddly enough, we found great inspiration in a little garden in southeastern England built in the shadow of a nuclear power plant. The late Derek Jarman's Dungeness garden was designed around a black and gold fisherman's cottage. It was full of wild plants and, like a desert garden, was well adapted to severe conditions. Dungeness is a harsh shingle plain that during some portions of the year gets about as much rainfall as Jordan. It is also often blasted with salt spray from the sea.

If there is such a thing, Dungeness is the desert of Britain. Jarman used native plants such as sea kale to give the garden a sense of place and to endure the challenging conditions. Like many Arizona gardens, it was mulched in gravel, with the plants set a proper distance from each other. Jarman's garden was embellished with witty antique spades, driftwood, and rounded flints that he found while beachcombing. This garden said Dungeness all over it. We wanted our garden, like Jarman's, to proudly display its regionalism.

Jarman called his garden "shaggy," but not in a pejorative sense. In his book *Derek Jarman's Garden* he wrote, "If it isn't shaggy, forget it." Jarman claimed that the greatest shaggy gardens are Christopher Lloyd's Great Dixter and Monet's garden at Giverny. But the garden we had in mind was probably considerably shaggier than Giverny. It could even be called stubbly or prickly.

We wanted to bring this peculiar and obsessive spirit of English gardening to Arizona. Elitist attitude could be checked at the door, but the garden should take some risks and not be afraid to be different. At the same time, we knew the garden would have an element of openness typically not found in British gardens. All in all, our garden would be a hybrid, something like the love child of Gertrude Jekyll and Edward Abbey, if such a thing were possible. Nature and Culture. Control and Wildness. We would give it a try.

Native plants such as ironwoods and agaves held a whole lot more interest for us than the traditional landscape plants used in Phoenix and Tucson in the 1970s and 80s. Plants like mulberries, Italian cypress, camellias, and gardenias look as out of place as chickens on the moon. They say nothing about the magical Sonoran Desert. Even worse, plants like gardenias are ill-suited for the intensity of our sunlight and our alkaline soil. Unless they are planted in a pot of rich acid soil and tended to like infants, they are bound to suffer the indignities of chlorosis, feebleness, and premature death.

My experience selling and caring for non-desert-adapted plants led us to a guiding design principle in our garden: plant only what thrives. We were not interested in growing a miserable yellowing azalea or pitiful magnolia for sentimental reasons. It was a "tough love" concept and a very American idea. As a nation, we value self-reliance in both people and plants. This tough bunch of Western plants would need a little help getting started but in short order would be pulling themselves up by their own boot-straps. Our plant palette was like a gang of unshaven gunslingers who cleaned up and dressed up to go into town a couple of times a year but for the most part avoided civilized society.

Trying to sell native plants in the nursery business sometimes felt like a losing proposition when I spoke with older nurserymen. At a national conference in Louisville, Kentucky, a seasoned nursery owner from the South approached after hearing me speak about native plants and said, "Son, it's all good and well if you want to sell a few wild weeds, but you're in for a long day if you're going to try to keep grannies from their gardenias." As much as I hated to admit it, he was partly right. Although the market for native plants was rapidly growing, especially the upscale market among young urban professionals, a lot of folks still wanted plants that reminded them of where they came from, and they were tough converts.

When I was out in the nursery helping customers, I tried to hide my feelings about particular plants and just give the customers the advantages and drawbacks of each variety; I tried to be cool and dispassionate, let the customers make their own decisions. But my heart wasn't in it—I *am* passionate about desert plants! Standing elbow to elbow with customers under a big blue canvas of sky, introducing them to some true Arizona natives, it was work I loved. I'm not selling Lucite paperweights, but the vestiges of a disappearing land.

These plants are treasures from the Pinacate Mountains, the Superstitions, the Catalinas, and the Pinaleños. Plants that proudly announce: Welcome to Arizona.

Save Water

In southern Arizona, self-reliance has a lot to do with water. In the thirty years I've lived in and around Arizona, I've seen wet years and dry years, but lately mostly dry years. During a flood year in the 1980s, I saw the Salt and Gila Rivers rise to the tops of their banks. Since the mid-1990s, I've never observed any water in the Gila River at all where Interstate 10 crosses it, heading north from Tucson. I explained to Zoë that the Gila was once a mighty river and that settlers in the late 1800s were often afraid to cross it. It even had a ferry. Looking at the bone-dry expanse of sand under the I-10 bridge, this seems like a tall tale. I don't think Zoë believes me.

Perhaps these are just my unscientific anecdotal observations, but the National Weather Service seems to agree with me, especially about the most recent years being some of the hottest and driest recorded. Whether people are causing this climate change or it is just part of a natural cycle, in Arizona 90 percent of our streams, rivers, and riparian areas have dried up or degraded because of excessive groundwater pumping. So what does this have to do with gardening? A lot of rare and interesting plants grow around the diminishing habitat of desert streams. Some of these plants may be lost before we can discover their charms in the garden. This may sound like a selfish reason to conserve wild streams and rivers—for the benefit of gardeners—but it's for the good of the plants too.

On a recent hike through one of Arizona's last perennial streams, Aravaipa Creek, I became keenly aware of the magic of desert water. I had been to Aravaipa at age sixteen, and I was pleased to discover that it hadn't changed a bit, I wanted to show it to Zoë, because I always remembered it as my favorite place on Earth. Within the narrow canyon I was mesmerized by the diversity of plant life. I saw walls of scarlet monkey flower and pockets of salvias, mints, and horsetail reed. Arizona sycamores and Arizona ashes towered overhead. Troops of coatimundis (raccoon-like creatures with lemur-like tails) marched by us with their tails straight up in the air. "What if the water dries up?" I thought. "What will happen to these wonderful plants and animals?"

In many ways a desert garden resembles a small, controlled riparian area. With just a little irrigation, you can grow some of the wild plants that might not be around in the wilds in a few more decades if the desert keeps getting drier. It's a sobering thought and one that causes us to rally around our last great wild places, but it also presents an exciting prospect—growing some rare desert plants in our own gardens.

In her book *Red,* Terry Tempest Williams says, "I want to keep my words wild so that even if the land and everything we hold dear is destroyed by short-sightedness and greed, there is a record of beauty and passionate participation by those who saw it coming."

Soft-tipped agave casts a bold shadow in the late afternoon.

For us, our wild yard would serve as an elegy to the land. If we love the great arboreal Sonoran Desert, why not plant some of it in our yards? If we are going to use precious fossil water pumped from underground aquifers to grow plants, why not plant the plants that make this place unique?

We knew we needed to conserve water, but we still wanted a lush and inviting garden. In order to resolve these conflicting desires we devised a rule for our plantings: we would not plant anything that required water more than once a week after establishment. This seemed like a fair trade-off. Many desert-adapted plants could thrive on this regimen. Even during the arid furnace of June, more than a few moderate-water-use plants, some of which we found thriving in Aravaipa Canyon, would find this schedule adequate.

It's a cliché, but the desert *is* a land of contrasts. During an August thunderstorm, I stood ankle deep in rushing water in the middle of our street. When it rains here it really rains. People get swept away trying to drive across washes that are usually dry. We even have a "stupid motorist law," which requires those who drive into rushing water to pay for their own rescues. In this crazy mixed-up desert we have the total absence of water and then an ineffable abundance. Intuitively, I knew that there had to be a way to capture this water.

And I'd be damned if we couldn't find a way to collect some of the thousands of gallons of rain that streamed off our roof after every monsoon storm.

Live Outside

Living outside seemed easy—get a barbecue, a table, and chairs, and begin cooking and eating outdoors. It was something millions of Americans did on mild summer evenings. Doing it with local flair was another story. We wanted to capture some of the strange and often contradictory flavor of Tucson in our outdoor spaces.

That spirit is often expressed in our local Mexican eateries. We are a town of taco stands, many of which—despite their nickname (roach coaches)—serve great food out of trucks with shiny chrome and fancy handpainted letters. Many serve a dozen different types of excellent tacos and burritos and can be a better bet than some place the chamber of commerce would send you to. My favorite restaurant is not quite a taco truck, but rather a tire shop. It is actually called Pepe's Tire Shop and Mexican Food, and I've been dying to get a flat in front of it, but so far I can only vouch for the green chile burro. Next to the food, the best thing about Pepe's is their decorative lettering and logos, all of which look handmade. Chief among these is an inexplicable shouting Confederate soldier.

We wanted a yard like Pepe's, not afraid to look different or even a little handmade. You have to admire the person who thought to combine a *llantería* (tire shop) with a restaurant: that's creativity. We wanted a lot of this kind of thinking in our garden.

This attitude took us down some strange paths. It turned a fairly normal brick patio into an outdoor living room complete with widescreen movie viewing, a crazy collection of garden accoutrements, and a love-nest alcove complete with futon and birdcage skeleton good-luck charm (more about this later). From March to November, we planned to spend big chunks of time out in the yard. We would eat breakfast and read the paper there in the morning, and unwind with iced tea after work.

Ultimately, we hoped that our yard would say a lot about who we are and where we live. We hoped it would articulate a unique vision of desert style.

Taco-stand style is as abundant as the green chile at Pepe's.

celebrate desert plants

celebrate desert plants—a palette for the new west

Unencumbered by notions of lawns and clipped hedges, we charged forward into the world of native plants.

Because so many of the wild plants we were using were new to horticulture, we felt like pioneers as we combined different plants in the garden. Had anyone ever planted desert lobelia next to golden columbine, with an ocotillo fence and sacred datura as a backdrop? We guessed not.

To be sure, this style of desert landscaping had its critics. Most desert plants are thorny and have small olive-green to silver leaves. As my mother-in-law remarked on a recent visit, "Everything has little leaves and thorns." If you've just moved here from Cleveland, you have to get used to some shades of green that are not the deep green you're accustomed to. Luckily, we were in the company of a good many desert plant evangelists, including a few prominent institutions, who were promoting Sonoran and Chihuahuan Desert plants as the best choices for desert yards. We were leaving the land of juniper and gardenias and coming into a new country full of ocotillo and Goodding's verbena. It was a good feeling, a little like hearing Curtis Mayfield sing about a train coming and then seeing that train pull into the station. In our case, the train would be filled with big palo verdes and mesquites, penstemons and agaves, barrel cacti and wildflower seeds. No doubt about it, we were getting on board.

Parry's penstemon glowing in the spring twilight (opposite); new Indian fig pad (inset); Mexican hat (pages 42–43).

The Importance of Desert Trees

When you come to the desert, you have to adjust your ideas of what trees are. Forget notions of thornless shade trees with single trunks and round, dark green canopies. In the desert Southwest, trees that look like lollipops are for children's drawings.

When I read Rick Darke's *The American Woodland Garden: Capturing the Spirit of the Deciduous Forest,* I was forced to confess that almost everything I know about the Eastern forest I learned from watching *The Last of the Mohicans* and reading Robert Frost poems. Although I am a professional plantsman and spend many hours a week designing, planting, and reading about gardens, I have almost no experience with the Eastern deciduous forest. To me, a forest of giant saguaro cacti is more familiar and comprehensible than a grove of river birches. In southern Arizona's lowlands, we have no maples, no birch, no hemlock or dogwood. What few trees we have seldom reach heights over twenty feet. In fact, many of the trees in the Southwest fall into a gray area between large shrubs and small trees.

In a lecture on their benchmark book, *Trees of Sonora, Mexico,* self-styled desert botanists and plant explorers Richard Felger and Matt Johnson defined trees as "plants that are big enough to climb." This seemed as good a definition as I was likely to find.

Using the "big enough to climb" definition, three main trees dominate the Sonoran Desert landscape: the palo verde, the mesquite, and the ironwood. If you walk out into the upper Sonoran Desert and you aren't in a really wet area, chances are that almost any tree you see that is more than eight feet high is going to be one of this trinity. So when I began to consider trees for my garden, I began with this holy trio (two of which have more than one species), followed by my other favorites, in no particular order.

Foothills palo verde (*Parkinsonia microphyllum,* formerly *Cercidium microphyllum*) In our front yard, the plant that has more impact on the garden than any other is a venerable forty-year-old salvaged foothills palo verde. A massive orange machine named "Goliath" delivered it. The tree came in a six-foot-high box, and the planting hole was dug using a Hitachi mini excavator. This violates my usual policy of digging my own holes, but given the size of the tree I made an exception.

These trees are not cheap; mine cost around $1,500, but it was money well spent. Since the foothills palo verde grows at what seems to be an agonizingly slow pace, buying an already mature salvaged tree made sense to an impatient gardener like me. Obviously, I couldn't afford, nor would it make sense, to buy all of my trees as giant salvaged specimens, but having one big boomer of a tree made quite a difference.

My palo verde is wonderfully twisted. It has seven main trunks that rise out of the ground like a lime-green candelabra. The tree has created an instant ecosystem and microclimate underneath it. Its filtered shade harbors hundreds of firewheel (*Gaillardia pulchella*), dogweed (*Thymophylla pentachaeta*), and Goodding's verbena. A large "horny toad" (horned lizard) has taken up residence under the tree, and a rock squirrel has made a home in an adjacent rock pile. I have planted several large agaves to take advantage of the ideal conditions the tree's canopy offers. As Mary Irish says in her book *Gardening in the Desert,* "shade is not a problem but a solution." The shade under my palo verde allows plants to thrive in a density that would be impossible in full sun without copious amounts of water. The numerous bean pods that fall from the tree in May and June also create a mulch that helps retain soil moisture around the tree.

Foothills palo verde in bloom.

Did I forget to mention that palo verdes have showy flowers? In the spring my foothills palo verde canopy is enveloped in a haze of butter-yellow flowers that match the paint on my front door. Right after the twisted green trunk, the flowers are the tree's second-best feature.

Besides the shade it provides and the glory of its spring flowers, the thing I appreciate most about my palo verde is that it shows respect for the landscape that existed before the bulldozers came through. Although my garden is not a revegetation project, using native plants connects the old with the new. It shows that the desert that existed in this place can be renewed. Natural patterns can be re-established.

Salvaged trees are trees that were in harm's way. They are trees that narrowly avoided a bulldozer blade. In Tucson, we have a preservation ordinance that requires native plants to be surveyed and evaluated for their viability before a parcel of land is bladed. This survey, conducted by a landscape architect or arborist, identifies which trees, cacti, and shrubs are valuable and are likely to survive and thrive after transplanting.

Salvaged trees, or even one salvaged tree, can solve a persistent problem in new residential gardens: new gardens often lack character. If salvaged trees are grouped with smaller trees they will mediate another problem in new landscapes: that all the plants look the same size.

Other notable palo verdes include our state tree, the blue palo verde, which has the showiest bright-yellow blossoms of all the palo verdes, as well as a host of new

Framed by foothills palo verdes, Deirdre and Zoë enjoy the late light.

thornless hybrids ('Desert Museum,' 'AZT Hybrid,' and 'Sonoran Emerald' among them).

Mesquite (*Prosopis* spp.)

> There is no straight to it, just this twisting and turning as it roasts under the sun… The tree is made for hard times.
>
> —Charles Bowden on Arizona native mesquite trees,
> *Blues for Cannibals*

Our velvet mesquite (*Prosopis juliflora*, formerly *P. velutina*) is a tree too tough to die. It has been cut down to fuel ore extraction, poisoned by ranchers hoping to eradicate the plant from grazing land, and made into charcoal for upscale restaurants. Once a tree that grew primarily in *bosques* (forests near watercourses or floodplains), it now grows in desert grasslands. Ironically, as the cattle eat the seedpods, digest the outer husk, and then deposit the seeds in a warm, damp pie (the perfect environment for good seed germination), grazing has helped to dramatically expand the mesquite's wild range.

As a landscape plant, the mesquite is a fine tree under which many desert plants will thrive on the soil made rich by the composted leaf litter.

In our garden, we inherited a large Chilean mesquite (*Prosopis chilensis*) that sits a few feet off our property line. I would have preferred a velvet (Arizona native) mesquite, because they have less of a habit of blowing over in high winds and their gray-green rather than bright green leaves look more at home with the surrounding desert. But since the neighboring Chilean mesquite was already a good size when we moved in, we decided to make the most of it.

Mesquite trees are as promiscuous as a single mother of six kids with six different fathers making an appearance on Jerry Springer, so it's hard to tell for sure what variety you actually have. Velvet and Chilean mesquites hybridize so freely that even the most skilled horticulturist often can't identify the resulting tree as wholly native or South American. The Chilean mesquite has been cultivated in Arizona extensively for more than twenty-five years. During that time, it has cross-pollinated with other mesquites (velvet mesquite, screwbean mesquite, Argentine mesquite, and Texas honey mesquite) to the point where it may or may not exhibit the characteristics of a Chilean. It doesn't help that most growers in the Southwest—myself included—know Chilean and Argentine mesquites only from what they've seen growing in Arizona.

It works like this: growers collect seeds from a Chilean mesquite whose form they like. The flowers that precede the seeds may have been pollinated by a bee that just visited a velvet or Argentine mesquite growing nearby. What the resulting tree will look like is anyone's guess. One thing nearly certain is that almost all mesquites that you purchase in the Southwest are, at least in some part, hybrids. This has led some horticulturists to call all Chilean- or Argentine-looking mesquites "South American hybrid mesquites." This name is accurate but unfortunate; it has none of the romance of "Chilean mesquite" or "Argentine mesquite." This name change has been slow to be adopted by nurseries, so if you're shopping for a non-native mesquite it is still likely to be labeled Chilean.

The Chilean mesquite is without a doubt the most popular landscape tree in southern Arizona, largely because it easily can grow four to six feet in a single growing season. Its dark brown to black trunk and feathery canopy also make it an obvious choice for many folks. It looks almost like an indigenous Sonoran Desert tree. Like a bright green umbrella arching over our brick patio, our Chilean mesquite is a fine tree for sitting under. We often enjoy its generous shade as we eat breakfast.

Palo blanco trunk.

Ironwood (*Olneya tesota*) Respect for the desert ironwood creeps up on you. My first experience with it was in San Carlos, Mexico, as a nine-year-old. I bought a small seal carved by Seri Indians, made from the dark heartwood of the desert ironwood. It was hard and smooth, and I rubbed it against my cheek as we drove home. In my teens, I walked the desert washes southeast of Phoenix, hunting quail with my father. There, ironwoods served as the preferred roosting site for quail. Hidden beneath the dense and thorny canopy, quail would not be flushed out until you were nearly standing under the tree.

It's not the flowers that make the ironwood so appealing. As garden author Judy Mielke says in an article published in *Arid Zone Times* newsletter, "It doesn't have the flashy bloom of palo verdes or the lush greenness of velvet mesquite, but its branches show the character gained through years—decades, really—of deliberate growth." The ironwood tree doesn't grow quickly, nor does it just sit there. Compared to similar-sized palo verdes planted in my front yard four years ago, an adjacent ironwood tree has grown about two-thirds as fast. When mature, it should reach a height and spread of about twenty-five feet.

Like most desert trees, the ironwood is typically multi-trunked, with branches low to the ground. It can be allowed to develop naturally or be pruned up into a more traditional tree form—no simple task, thanks to an abundance of stout, half-inch curved spines. Like most desert legumes, ironwoods drop a fair amount of litter; that considered, they are still a good choice to shade patios. Hardy only to 20 degrees Fahrenheit, the ironwood was traditionally used as an indicator plant for where citrus would grow. As an evergreen tree, ironwood serves well to anchor the landscape through all seasons, and its dramatic character can create a focal point in entries and other high-visibility areas.

Recently, the beauty of the ironwood tree has been celebrated by the creation of Ironwood National Monument about twenty-five miles northwest of Tucson. Even with all this good press, though, the ironwood is seldom used as a landscape tree. It is without a doubt the finest native shade tree for the low desert. It has a dense evergreen foliage, can live up to three hundred years, and boasts stunning gray-green leaves with pale lavender or (occasionally) rose-colored flowers that turn into seedpods containing edible beans reminiscent of peanuts. My favorite thing about the ironwood is its multi-stemmed silvery trunk.

One regret we had about living on such a small lot was that we didn't have room for an ironwood. The ironwood can get to be a good-sized tree and needs room to grow. I considered taking down our Chilean mesquites and replacing them with three salvaged ironwoods, but I couldn't bring myself to fell trees whose green lacework canopies were already casting dappled shade on our patio.

What we did have room for were very small and slender trees. We took a walk on the wild side and planted trees from central Sonora, Mexico, called palo blancos (or in Mexico, *palos blancos*).

Palo blanco (*Acacia willardiana*) The first time I saw palo blancos in the wild was on a trip to Alamos, Mexico. We were just south of Hermosillo, and I was looking out the window at an orange, boulder-studded mountain. Against the red rocks, the white trunks stood out like vertical slash marks made by a painter's brush. In these unbelievably harsh conditions (a baking rock mountainside), the palo blanco dominated the mountain. It was the only visible tree, its slight weeping canopy blowing in a desiccating wind.

Because the palo blanco is the most subtle and elegant of all the low desert trees, we have given it a prominent spot in our yard. In the enclosed back garden, we planted a grove of palo blancos whose weeping forms will drape over our ramada seating area. Because of its most endearing feature, its scroll-like white peeling bark, I like to call this tree the river birch of the desert. Not tolerant of extreme cold, the palo blanco should be planted in warm microclimates and protected when young. The tree is so slender that the city of Paradise Valley, Arizona, recommends it in a master plan for the landscaping along streets and in median strips as narrow as five feet.

In my own garden, four palo blancos have withstood two nights of 17-degree cold with only minor tip damage. In intermediate-elevation deserts, planting this tree carries some risk, but what gardener doesn't have a secret desire to beat the odds, to grow a tree in one or even two zones colder than a reference recommends? I know I do, especially when it's a tree as charming and truly Sonoran as the palo blanco.

A coworker of mine, horticulturist Eric Clark, loves the coldest winter nights in the desert. He is fond of telling gardeners who come into the nursery with a pitiful frost-blackened *Ficus nitida* branch, "I told you it would be too cold for that."

In his zeal, he has even warned me about the risks of growing a palo blanco on the far east side of Tucson. But with visions of white peeling bark and the most airy and imperceptible canopy imaginable, I look him in the eye and say, "I'll take my chances."

Claret cup cactus bloom.

Sweet acacia (*Acacia farnesiana*) and **Catclaw acacia** (*Acacia greggii*)—"The Second Scent of the Desert"… Although the acacias are not part of the trinity of desert trees, they are easily the fourth most common species of large plants in the Sonoran Desert. The sweet acacia has a mysterious, dry, sweet smell that is not cloying— an addictive smell that expresses the clean delight of spring in the Southwest. After the creosote bush, acacias have the next most recognizable scent in the desert. Even Thomas Jefferson grew *Acacia farnesiana* in a Monticello greenhouse in order to enjoy its perfume. Indigenous Oaxacan people use the bean pods as a

Worn-out rake, 8-gauge yellow electrical wire, ocotillo fence.

black dye, and perfumers use oils from the bloom as an ingredient in *eaux de toilettes*.

As with the mesquite, much horticultural confusion surrounds the sweet acacia, which can make it hard to buy the tree you want. Here's what I know from observing several hundred growing in landscapes. There are two recognizable forms of the sweet acacia: one is short and tends to bloom in both fall and spring; the other is a much larger tree that seems to bloom only in spring.

The sweet acacia rarely occurs north of the border in Arizona and California, but its shrubbier cousin the catclaw acacia is widespread. Catclaw acacia gets its name from its recurved thorns. It produces a very fragrant flower and can be shaped into a fine small landscape tree.

For no good reason, the catclaw acacia is hardly ever used in residential landscapes. In the upper Sonoran region, it is the true second scent of the desert, more simple and clean than any cosmetic-counter fragrance. As you drive north out of Phoenix on Interstate 17, you will see the catclaw acacia on the roadside and in the washes. At freeway speed, it almost looks like an ironwood tree with its silver-gray bark and gray-green leaves. Then you look again and think, "Hey, it is way too cold here for ironwood." Catclaw acacia is cold-hardy to 0 degrees Fahrenheit and often grows in transition areas between low desert and high country.

Even in midwinter, when the promise of acacia blooms is weeks away, I anticipate the perfume of those blossoms by eating desert or "catclaw" honey. The earthy sweet smell comes through in the taste. Yet I can't help but wonder if there will be catclaw honey for my grandkids. With the pace of development encroaching on acres and acres of desert each day, it seems that desert beekeeping, at best a marginal existence, may gradually just fade away. Every beekeeper I've ever met seems to be near seventy years old. Who will carry on this sweet tradition? Since desert honey from catclaw acacia and mesquite puts other honey to shame, I'm going to keep on buying it even if it costs a little more. If we create a demand, maybe the bee-keepers will keep making desert honey.

At our house, I tried my best to fit a catclaw acacia into the plan, but our little lot simply had no room for any more trees. We did have a sweet acacia already, and I planned to take full advantage of it. It's the shorter type. In November and March it's cloaked with gold puffball blossoms. It overhangs an adobe wall in our rear garden like a twisted, airy beach umbrella. Its sweet and dusky scent blows into the house through open windows and can be smelled for blocks away. The small, bright-yellow flowers are attractive in their own right, and since the tree is semi-evergreen it never looks altogether bare.

Ocotillo (*Fouquieria splendens*)

Ocotillos fifteen feet tall grew along the way; in March and April each spiderlike branch would be tipped with a scarlet cone of tiny flowers, looking from a distance like flames.

—Edward Abbey, *Cactus Country*

Although climbing it would be the work of a true masochist, in my book the ocotillo (or coach whip) is a tree. With its long, upright thorny branches and extreme vase shape, it is easily the most architectural tree in any garden, with the possible exception of its Baja California cousin, the weird and wonderful upside-down green carrot of the boojum tree. In the spring our ocotillo puts out orange/red tubular flowers at the ends of its branches that attract hummingbirds migrating northward. The flowers are often followed by profuse leaf growth that makes the plant look twice its size. With the onset of the dry fore-summer, the leaves fall off and the ocotillo goes dormant. When the

summer rains come, the ocotillo transforms itself into a leafy plant once again, often seemingly within the space of a few hours. If there is a plant that more quickly adapts to the changing conditions of the desert, I haven't seen it.

When I was shopping for my ocotillo, I faced a small moral dilemma. Almost all of the ocotillos currently sold in Arizona come from Texas. Now, I don't have anything against plants from Texas or people with "Don't mess with Texas" bumper stickers, but something bothered me about all those cattle trucks full of ocotillos rolling through El Paso and Las Cruces on their way to Tucson, Phoenix, and Scottsdale. According to my rough calculations, about three-quarters of all the ocotillos that once grew in west Texas are now planted in north Scottsdale and in the foothills of the Santa Catalina Mountains in Tucson. I'm unsure if this is a bad thing. I mean, at least half of them survived transplanting. They can now grow in a place with no threat of a rancher ripping them out of the ground and just dumping them. To top it all off, Arizona is looking more and more beautiful with thousands of new ocotillos flowing into the state every year. Is it our fault if Texas has flimsy native-plant exportation laws? Still, I couldn't help but imagine a ranch up on a ridge next to Big Bend National Park denuded of all its ocotillos save a few pitiful stragglers too small for market. Ocotillo brokers assured me that they were harvesting only a percentage of the ocotillos on any one ranch, but I still wondered what those ranches looked like. To top it off, many of the same ocotillo brokers were now selling giant beaked yucca, New Mexico agave (*Agave parryi* var. *neomexicana*), and horse crippler cacti.

One afternoon, a rancher pulled up to the nursery with an entire semi-tractor cattle trailer full of large and exquisite New Mexico agaves. I climbed up to the top deck and looked out on a rectangle of hundreds of gray rosettes. It was more *neomexicana* than I had seen in my entire life—beautiful ghostly gray rosettes with black margins and tips that I knew I could sell in the nursery if I properly potted and cared for them. I reluctantly bought a dozen for way too cheap a price, but I still wondered about the west Texas ranch they came from. My colleague Marc White, a skilled and sometimes hot-headed horticulturist from New Mexico State University with little patience for what he called "Texas plant thieves," said, "Who do they think they are? Are these public lands they are taking these plants off?" It was a good question and one I can't really answer without going to Texas and seeing these operations myself.

I don't want to give you the wrong impression. Although they were pretty well done with cows by the time I came along, I do come from a family of ranchers. My grandfather founded the Kyrene Land and Cattle Co. in what is now suburban Phoenix. In general, most ranchers have an intimacy with the land they work. I know one rancher who plants hundreds of pounds of blue grama grass seed on his land and rotates his cattle around so they actually help the high desert grassland to flourish. To buy my ocotillo from Texas, I had to trust that I was dealing with an honest land steward.

In August of 2003, two cactus-growing friends of mine showed me an alternative to Texas ocotillos. They were both growing ocotillos from seed. Between the two of them, there would be a few thousand two- or three-foot-tall five-gallon ocotillos for sale in just a couple of years. I got very excited and promised to buy all they could produce. We sell well over a thousand ocotillos each year at the nursery, and if at least a portion of those came from seed rather than Texas ranches, I would be mighty pleased.

In the meantime, I needed an ocotillo in my yard and had no choice but to buy a made-in-Texas product. I suppose all of us impatient Arizona desert rats are part of the problem. We don't want to wait for the little ocotillo seedling to mature. We would rather buy an eight-footer from Texas, so the Texas plant brokers are just filling a market demand. What kind of environmentalist does this make me? Still, my beautiful eight-foot-tall specimen occupies prime real estate in my front garden. And when those Arizona-grown seedlings are ready, I'll be sure to promote them as best I can.

Saguaro (*Carnegiea gigantea*) Although technically not a tree, the saguaro cactus is *the* charismatic megaflora of the Sonoran Desert and a plant with a curious relationship to the trinity of desert trees. Old saguaros that seem to preside over shorter desert trees actually rely on them to nurture their young; juvenile saguaros grow in high numbers under the canopies of the foothills palo verde, ironwood, and mesquite. These "nurse trees" protect the infant saguaros from extreme heat and provide slightly higher soil moisture than would be available on open desert. As the decades go by, the nurse tree is overtaken by the saguaros, which can reach heights of more than fifty feet.

I like to think of the saguaro as a Greek Doric column with its tapered base and fluted ribs. Architectural in the extreme, the saguaro looks capable of supporting the Parthenon. As with olive trees in Greece, you plant saguaros for your grandchildren. The slow-growing plant takes thirty to thirty-five years to reach sexual maturity (that is, to flower and produce fruit).

In our yard, there seemed no better location for a saguaro than under our foothills palo verde. Since saguaros transplant more successfully when less than six feet tall, we started a four-footer salvaged from an adjacent development. Using an old scrap of carpet and a garden hose, Deirdre and I muscled the little guy into place, taking care to orient the plant's south side as it had been in the wild, to avoid sunburn. After a few summer rains the little saguaro plumped up and the palo verde set out a full complement of tiny green leaves. They seemed a happy couple.

Tenaza (*Harvardia pallens,* formerly *Pithecellobium pallens*) The last tree we put in our desert garden was a tenaza. This thorny little Chihuahuan Desert tree has a deep green, densely branched structure, but what it's really good at is blooming wave after wave of fragrant white puffball flowers. We planted one next to our circular brick patio in front of the house so we could smell the sweet musky vanilla scent on summer mornings. I like to cook up some eggs and sit out there reading the paper in an Adirondack chair beneath the tenaza. This tree is just large enough to provide shade to sit in—and when you think about it, that's about all you can ask of a desert tree. A little bit of shade can make a desert garden possible.

Agaves—Living Sculptures in the Yard

Agaves, or century plants, are Southwestern icons. Imagine a Western movie without a Mexican bandit drinking from a bottle of mescal (which is made from the roasted and fermented agave heart, as is tequila). All agaves are New World plants, with the majority of species native to Mexico and the U.S. Southwest. Individual agaves may live for two or more decades; then, in a final, spectacular surge of energy, the plant sends up a single flower stalk that can rise to thirty feet high. Many people find the death of an agave tragic: "You mean to tell me it blooms only once and dies?" But to me, the infrequency and audacity of the agave's bloom

Trio of mescal ceniza in yellow pots illuminated by late afternoon sun.

Soft-tipped agave.

proof infidels cannot escape the power of such a magic name, the glamour of that sinister reputation, the occult touch of all those bored and restless haunts, the spirits of the place."

I have been on the Reavis Ranch Trail three times in my life—as a Boy Scout, as a college student, and most recently as a middle-aged father traveling with my own father. That last trip was the first time I really paid close attention to the agaves along the trail. It was late spring, and Palmer's agaves were blooming en masse. Our hike was a journey through a forest of ten- to eighteen-foot-high chartreuse flower stalks. We walked next to a carpet of Mexican gold poppy and camped in a slot canyon draped with patches of golden columbine and scarlet monkey flower, but what I remember most is how the agave stalks glowed in the afternoon light.

It is safe to say that I can blame the Reavis Ranch Trail for much of my ongoing obsession with agaves. Seeing agaves in the wild has made me wild for them in my garden. Surrounded by fine-leafed desert flowers and shrubs, agaves add instant year-round structure to any yard. Their symmetrical rosette shape adds order to adjacent desert plants that are more unruly. I began to think of the agave as a giant stylized rose, more beautiful and infinitely tougher than any hybrid tea rose, but still well-mannered. The agave—a civilized, important plant in American desert landscapes—can be used to keep the shaggy hordes of native shrubs in check.

I recently gave a group of English gardeners a tour of Arizona gardens, and the one thing they couldn't get over was how we planted agaves directly in the ground. Evidently, agaves are strictly a potted plant on the other side of the pond (probably because too much water sitting around the roots would cause rotting). They were green with envy over Arizona's in-ground agaves.

As I thought about the British, spending countless hours each fall and spring schlepping huge potted agaves in and out of greenhouses, it occurred to me

and impending death make the plant that much more mysterious and alluring.

My journey into the world of agaves began in a mountain range near Mesa, Arizona. Off a famously rough dirt road called the Apache Trail, a double-track path called the Reavis Ranch Trail heads into the remote and rocky Superstition Wilderness, winding around peninsular rock formations and up into the high elevations of the rugged volcanic mountains.

I've always been a sucker for a good place name, and maybe that's partly why I like the Superstition Mountains so much. As Ed Abbey said in *Cactus Country,* "Nobody gets in and out of the Superstition Mountains *completely* untouched. Even the most hex-

that here in the Southwest we live in an agave gardener's paradise. Considering the multitude of uses for agaves in my Arizona yard, I could hardly contain myself. I already had the collection of potted agaves we had grown on our apartment balcony—plus a list of species I wanted to add.

I began at the entrance to the house, where I placed green soft-tipped agaves (*Agave polyacantha*) in matching square yellow pots on either side of the front door. This was my salute to the British gardeners, with their tendency to place urns of agaves on either side of pathways. This was about the only salute I would give to the Europeans. At any rate, it seemed to suit my front porch just fine. Some people might consider placing agaves near a foot-traffic area hazardous. After all, many species are armed with sharp saw-like teeth along the margins of their leaves, and most have sharp terminal tips. But a few agaves, like *Agave polyacantha,* have softer tips, making them admirably suited for planting near walkways. Besides, my *polyacantha* was perfect for the shady conditions on my front porch, where it would also receive some protection from hard frosts.

Some mothers are concerned about planting agaves in areas where children might pass. My usual reply is that unless children are terribly slow, they will get stuck only once. My own daughter, Zoë, who once got poked as a curious toddler, now navigates around my spiny collections with no trouble at all. She will even help me plant agaves.

What agave gardeners soon realize is that these plants are relatively easy to handle. They have no small hair-like needles (glochids) like the ones you find on many cactus species. As long as you watch for the terminal points and handle the plant by its roots, you will rarely receive mortal injury.

I wanted to bring some of the same yellow that I had used on my front door and agave pots into the garden. Oddly enough, I found that yellow in the leaf margins

of a giant granddaddy of an agave, *Agave americana* var. *marginata* (commonly called the variegated century plant). This plant can get scary-big, which to be honest is part of the fun. It would not be unusual for one of these to get over seven feet high. I planted three of them in an asymmetrical triangle that straddled both sides of the pathway to the front door. The century plant—the largest and most commonly grown of all the agaves—is now found in warm parts of the world from Africa to Australia. In some arid locales it has escaped from gardens and gone wild. *Agave americana* comes in many varieties, from the standard blue-gray foliage (*A. americana*) to many variegated versions, including some with yellow stripes (*A. americana* var. *marginata*).

Some agave connoisseurs look down their noses at *Agave americana* because it is so commonly used. In southern Arizona, it also has a tendency to get infested by the snout-nose agave weevil, which can kill a large agave in short order. I have witnessed my share of

White stripe agave in a Cuban cigar canister.

infestations, and what appears to happen is this: the female beetle pokes her nose into the flesh of an agave leaf to test for sugars; if the sugar level is right she lays eggs, which turn into fat white grubs that eat the roots of the agave. You do not notice the problem until your agave leaves begin to collapse and turn brown. Once this happens, the end is near. Infestation is relatively common in *Agave americana,* so much so that it is rare to see them bloom before they get the beetle. On the bright side, you can spray for the beetles, and even if your plant gets infested and dies, *Agave americana* produces numerous pups or offsets (baby agaves) around the base of the plant, which usually survive and can be used to replace it.

Despite its shortcomings, there are no real substitutes for this hulk of a plant, especially the variegated forms. And frankly, I find the size and shape of *Agave americana* irresistible.

On a recent trip to the small town of Bisbee in southeastern Arizona, Deirdre and I were walking along the steep streets looking at yards. We were nearly at the top of a hill and were admiring a fine garden next to an abandoned wooden shack when a summer monsoon storm began in earnest. For a while, we hunkered down on the leeward side of a bakery truck parked on the street. When the wind changed directions, we were forced onto the rickety porch of the shack. The rain lasted longer than a typical storm, so we entertained ourselves by seeing who could take the best picture with our digital camera. Adjacent to the porch was a group of *Agave americanas* next to an urn fountain. Wet with rain, the silver agaves looked metallic—almost like aluminum.

All things considered, *Agave americana* var. *marginata* was a big bad plant with yellow racing stripes that matched my front door. Damn the snout-nose agave weevil and full steam ahead, I was going to plant three of them.

In the almost-as-big-as-a-house agave category, I knew of one other blue-gray specimen I had to have: Weber's agave (*Agave weberi*). This agave is big and smooth-skinned, with no barbs along the margins of its leaves. Deirdre and I wanted to plant three of these around the arch of our brick patio. Their silver-blue foliage provides an impeccable backdrop for green-and-red plants such as bat-faced cuphea (*Cuphea llavea*). I found three five-gallon specimens at the nursery that within a year and a half were nearly three feet tall and just as wide. Eventually, these agaves would grow too big for the space and would have to be moved, but for a time, they looked like big blue living sculptures.

For medium-sized plants we started with a southern Arizona standard, Parry's agave. For a landscape agave these silver plants with black spines are hard to beat. They tolerate both heat and cold (down to at least 5 degrees Fahrenheit) and look fabulous poking up among wildflowers such as desert marigold, Goodding's verbena, and sacred datura. We planted three Parry's agaves in a triangular pattern adjacent to the path to our front porch and sowed wildflower seeds around them. We planted two distinct varieties—a regular Parry's and a shorter variety that grows in the shape of an artichoke and shares that name. This truncated artichoke agave is much sought after, especially a particular clone from the Huntington Botanical Garden in the Los Angeles metro area called Gentry's agave (after Howard Gentry, pioneer agave expert), which has elongated, deep-red tips and ghostly blue-gray foliage in a perfect rosette.

Both of these forms of Parry's agave work with nearly any combination of flowering plants and tolerate nearly any soil. I planted a trio of artichoke agaves in red cube-shaped pots.

Firewheel seedhead.

The back yard required medium-sized agaves, deeper green in color. We chose a rare sharkskin agave hybrid (*Agave scabra* × *ferdinand-regis*) for its thick fleshy leaves, with some lower-growing Queen Victoria agaves down in front.

The hottest little collector agave on the market, the Queen Victoria is causing a stir among Southwest gardeners. I myself have lost my head over these small green-and-white striped wonders. In its native Mexico, this species grows along the steep, rocky canyons and hillsides of Durango and Nuevo León. It has been given a "danger of extinction" designation, which has bolstered its stature among collectors. It also seems to be featured in every other Tucson and Phoenix home and garden magazine article, which has introduced the plant to a large market of desert dwellers. Because of recent laws passed in Mexico, there are also rumors of seed shortages, which may make the plant even more sought after than it already is. Fortunately, many Tucson cactus and succulent growers are propagating Queen Victoria from offsets, which can be numerous in potted plants.

The fact is, the unusually tight rosette shape and deep green leaves with white markings are mesmerizing enough without all the hype about its being rare and protected and the perfect plant to set on your patio. In

Queen Victoria agave.

our garden, Queen Victoria agaves are the crown jewels. We have no fewer than twelve, and that seems an insufficient number. My favorite two are polar opposites.

The first is a respectable "old man" nearly as big as a beach ball, for which I paid the fine sum of zero. I was driving home from lunch one day and noticed a Bobcat (a small earth-mover) pushing a heap of rare and beautiful cacti and agaves into a mound. At first, I was as distraught as someone happening upon the mass execution of close friends. It was enough to make me cry, if not for the salvage opportunity. Within ten minutes, I had spoken to the owner of the garden, a woman who had bought the house and garden from a University of Arizona horticulturist, and I learned that the cactus garden did not suit her tastes, so she was ripping it out. I secured permission to salvage anything I wanted from the pile. To my great delight, I pulled out a large and nearly perfect Queen Victoria and saved it from an ignominious end at the dump. I called some friends, and we cleaned the pile of all its treasures like greedy pirates after booty. I potted my new acquisition in a large yellow pot, where it has happily roosted for several years. It is worth a lot of money now, so I can only pray that no one will steal it, because I fear that they will not love it as much as I do.

My other favorite Queen Victoria is a little hybrid called *Agave victoriae-reginae* var. 'Himesanoyuki' (Snow Princess)—a dwarf selection with intricate white markings, and smaller than a tennis ball. I keep it in a curious square pot with a Japanese design that was painted in a village near San Miguel de Allende, Mexico. This odd "East meets West" pot seems to house my Snow Princess elegantly.

Another excellent small- to medium-sized landscape variety is the mescal ceniza (*Agave colorata*), which appears to have been dusted with powdered sugar. We planted three of these in yellow pots that we placed on a little adobe seat wall. *Agave colorata* has become fairly popular in southern Arizona but remains rare elsewhere. It is reportedly cold-hardy to 5 degrees Fahrenheit, and I've heard rumors that it has been grown successfully in Denver. My favorite thing about *Agave colorata* is its color and the patterns on the leaves. As it grows and its leaves unfold, the imprint of the outer leaves is left on the inner leaves—something horticulturists call a bud impression. The leaves are wide with deeply serrated edges. They have a dusty silvery-blue color and rough texture that makes them unique in the agave world. Certainly these are the only agave that appear to have powdered sugar sprinkled on them.

All this talk about agaves has gotten me thinking about agaves in the wild again. Late this spring will be a good time to go back up the Reavis Ranch Trail. Although the agave collection in my garden gives me great pleasure, I know of no substitute for hiking through a hillside punctuated by hundreds of agave bloom stalks—and out there, no one mourns the loss of an agave. It is a natural process with its own charms. As the agave dies its flesh turns brilliant shades of red, yellow, and chartreuse. It is a vivid end. After all, who would not want to die like the agave—to live for decades to one purpose, gathering all your strength, and sending up a thirty-foot spire full of offspring—a symbol of utter defiance in the dying light?

Although a dying agave can be visually sublime, some biologists say that agaves in the wild are dying faster than normal because stress from prolonged drought has made them more susceptible to snout-nose weevil infestation. As yet, this evidence is anecdotal, and we can only care for the agaves in our gardens and pray for rain for their wild kin.

Since I can't be on the trail most days, I count on the agaves in my garden to make me happy. I never tire of their form and like to look at them in every season. A lot of folks confuse agaves with aloes, which bloom predictably every year without dying. The aloes are all African plants and include some fine species, but somehow they seem less appropriate in Southwestern gardens. For one thing, aloes can't take the coldest nights in the interior deserts without frost protection. If you forget to cover them on a really cold night, the next morning you may be faced with a slick of aloe vera jelly where your aloes used to be. Since they have fewer thorns than agave, and some species are used to treat sunburn, aloes seem like a plant Arnold Schwarzenegger would plant around his pool in Los Angeles.

Although I have a several clumps of a small aloe hybrid called 'Blue Elf' growing in the ground, I think aloes tend to look best in pots in American desert gardens.

Out in Arizona, Utah, New Mexico, Colorado, Texas, and yes, even California, you need to plant agaves among your penstemons. You can begin with just one whose color and shape you like, that grows well in your zone. As you use your pick or digging bar or jackhammer in some godforsaken rocky Western

Variegated century plant, Parry's penstemon, and ocotillo fence.

soil, you can rest assured that the agave you are about to plant will find a way to root in. It wants to survive at least as much as you do. This hot, arid world is the only one it knows. After you firm up the dirt around its roots, stand back and admire your work. Smile. You're a bona fide American agave gardener.

Penstemons—Towers of Hummingbird Power

I've always found beauty in odd places, but perhaps never more so than the time I found several acres of hot-pink Parry's penstemon growing along the fringes of a Motorola semiconductor plant parking lot in suburban Phoenix. My mother and I stumbled onto this field early one April. We parked the car and walked a ways out into the waving spires of fluorescent pink suspended above glaucous blue foliage. Obviously, someone had planted these penstemons as a seed crop. These were well-watered, vigorous plants. The air was buzzing with big black carpenter bees and hummingbirds drunk with pollen. The effect was mesmerizing. At that moment, standing in the hot-pink haze of four-foot-high spikes, I was done for. I had fallen hard for the charms of this spunky Arizona-native plant.

Falling for a pink flower was unusual for me. On that side of the spectrum, I tended toward fire-engine red flowers rather than blooms the color of a blushing maiden, and I was also more likely to become enamored of a strange agave than a flower. But Parry's penstemon was such a flamboyant pink that in my mind I nearly counted it red.

I went absolutely nuts for the plant. I wanted at least one Parry's penstemon in every square yard of my garden. Something about the combination of pink flowers against blue foliage was irresistible. If there is a fairer perennial plant in the desert, I have yet to see it.

A friend gave me a mason jar half-full of the tiny black Parry's penstemon seeds shaped like tiny shark's teeth, and I squandered them all over my Tucson garden. It was enough seed for several seasons, but I greedily sowed the entire jar on one fall day. It was like eating a gallon of Mississippi Mud chocolate ice cream at a single sitting.

I had grown penstemons before, in my Great Basin garden in Utah, and they had been a pleasure there as well. In fact, with 70 of the world's 272 penstemon specimens native to Utah, the state was the epicenter of wild penstemons. In Utah, I had much luck with many species of lower-growing rock-garden types, as well as with a few of the showier, taller species, but I could not grow Parry's worth a darn. It was a little too cold there. My Arizona garden would change my luck at growing the showstoppers of the penstemon world. Arizona can't boast the most penstemon species, but it is home to many of the most flamboyant varieties (Parry's among them).

The architecture of penstemons—or hummingbird skyscrapers, as Zoë calls them—consists of clumps of rosette leaves at ground level, with long vertical flower spikes shooting up through the leaves. The flowers themselves bloom on the spike at a more-or-less ninety-degree angle to the spike, depending on the species. Each tubular bloom is perfectly designed for the business end of the hummingbird's beak.

As far as I was concerned, three penstemon species stood head and shoulders above the others: Parry's, superb, and firecracker. These would form the backbone of the penstemon collection in my Tucson garden. Other species, such as canyon penstemons and the fragrant giant snapdragons (also called Palmer's penstemons), would fill niches where I had a little more shade. In addition, I included a smaller red variety, rock penstemon, where I needed lower-growing plants near a path.

In the late fall after I had sown my mason jar of Parry's penstemon seeds, tiny dark green rosettes began to push their way up out of the hard alkaline soil. To the casual non-gardener observer, these unremarkable seedlings might even be mistaken for weeds. To me, the germination of my penstemon seeds was nothing short of a small miracle.

All winter, I observed the progress of my crop. The rosettes became larger and leafier but still remained rather unremarkable. I carefully weeded out crowded plants, giving each plant enough room to achieve greatness. I paid close attention to the condition of the leaves.

In January, I noticed that some of the Parry's penstemons on the north side of the house were getting too much shade and suffered from powdery mildew, a malady that more often affects roses. I moved many of these plants into the full sun, where they thrived. In the shady holes left behind, I planted canyon penstemon, a plant accustomed to darker recesses. It has performed very well.

Showtime

Because of flowers such as penstemons, spring is the showiest time of year in southern Arizona. Although we don't grow as many bulbs as northern gardeners do, the natural landscape glows with the jewel-like colors of wildflowers. In the wild part of my garden, I was trying to simulate and enhance the glowing luminescence of the spring desert.

In very early spring, my wild garden begins with a trio of bloomers: hot-pink Parry's penstemon, true-blue desert bluebells, and bright yellow brittlebush. This pink, blue, and yellow may well be the best color combination in the garden the entire year. Brittlebush

The surreal glow of Parry's penstemon in the evening sun.

A carpenter bee visits a Parry's penstemon blossom.

makes an excellent foil for Parry's penstemon, with its yellow flowers hovering above its silver leaves.

The hot pink of Parry's penstemon also complements the green trunk and yellow flowers of the foothills palo verde and the silver foliage of the desert marigold (*Baileya multiradiata*). This show lasts one to two months depending on the weather, usually in March and April. On Zoë's birthday, March 31, I can always count on getting good photos of the spring penstemon show. On evenings in March and April, with the camera steadied on a tripod, I wait until the wind dies and the flowers glow.

Spring is brief and intense, but it underscores the magical transformations the desert is capable of. It is followed by a season that we call the dry foresummer. During this time, the penstemon stalks finish blooming and harden. They turn brown and become a source of seeds for finches, sparrows, and wrens, who perch on the stalks and bend them over like pole-vaulters.

Like all desert plant life, penstemons have a strategy for coping with drought: they go into a semi-dormant state during the dry fore-summer and summer. On firecracker penstemon, the bulk of the rosette may dry up and look dead, only to surprise you in fall with fresh new leaves emerging from the base.

I find that now, in my fifteenth year of serious gardening, my passion for penstemons has not faded. I patrol the rosettes of Parry's in the wild front area of my bungalow each winter. As spring approaches and the bloom stalks begin to push up, I can hardly contain my excitement. This beautiful plant, this hummingbird skyscraper, has made itself at home all over my garden. Surely, I'm a wealthy man, filthy rich in hot-pink architectural towers, favored by hummingbirds both domestic and foreign.

Caution: Wildflowers Ahead

Last October, my friend Carrie Nimmer called and said, "I've got the stuff—it's time to bomb."

"Huh?" I answered.

"I've got your wildflower seeds; we're going to bomb your garden."

"Great," I said. "Bring them this weekend."

We had begun seeding the front garden every year with a variety of desert wildflower seeds, with steadily increasing success. I already had good stands of hot-pink Parry's penstemon and golden desert marigold, but Carrie brought me new treasures such as Mexican gold poppy and true-blue succulent lupine. Carrie, a former professional ballet dancer turned Phoenix-based landscape designer, is best known for her knockout desert wildflower displays.

When we work in my garden together, she calls out my name in an exaggerated Buffalo, New York, accent

Scott's top twenty-one favorite desert wildflowers

1 Parry's penstemon (*Penstemon parryi*)
2 desert bluebells (*Phacelia campanularia*)
3 desert marigold (*Baileya multiradiata*)
4 brittlebush (*Encelia farinosa*—the only shrub on this list)
5 Mexican gold poppy (*Eschscholtzia mexicana*)
6 California poppy (*Eschscholtzia californica*)
7 firewheel (*Gaillardia pulchella*)
8 globemallow (*Sphaeralcea ambigua*)
9 Goodding's verbena (*Glandularia gooddingii*)
10 dogweed (*Thymophylla pentachaeta*)
11 a trio of lupines: desert lupine (*Lupinus sparsiflorus*), succulent lupine (*L. succulentus*), and Arizona lupine (*L. arizonicus*)

12 tufted evening primrose (*Oenothera caespitosa*)
13 spreading fleabane (*Erigeron divergens*)
14 firecracker penstemon (*Penstemon eatoni*)
15 giant snapdragon (*Penstemon palmeri*)
16 Mexican hat (*Ratibida columnaris*)
17 devil's claw (*Proboscidea parviflora*)
18 prairie zinnia (*Zinnia grandiflora*)
19 Arizona poppy (*Kallstroemia grandiflora*)
20 desert senna (*Senna covesii*)
21 sacred datura (*Datura wrightii*)

Twin desert bluebells.

when she needs my help or disapproves of my plant placement. "Scaawt!" she says.

Carrie showed up at the house carrying a big cellophane bag filled with smaller cellophane bags. The small bags had card stock folded and stapled across their tops, with the species of each type of seed handwritten on each. To me it looked like she had used an extra-fine-point Uniball 0.5 mm pen to write the names. If Carrie does anything, she does it with flair.

Most of the seed Carrie gives me is clean and comes labeled with the botanical name of the species—*Lupinus sparsiflorus,* for example. But because Carrie often collects her own seed, it is sometimes not clean. That is,

it still might have the pods, husks, or other chaff attached to the seed.

The last batch of seed she brought had a lot of unclean seed and included some mystery mixes with warnings on the labels: "Dirty Mojave Mix," "Scary Sonoran Stuff," and "Prickly So. Cal. Seeds." Planting seed mixes with these names required great faith in Carrie's taste in wildflowers.

The seed packet labeled "Dirty Mojave Mix" got my attention right away. It sounded like the music a DJ would play in a sleazy Tijuana bar that specialized in helping college kids lose their virginity. The "Scary Sonoran Stuff" sounded like some powerful psychotropic drug that would induce visions of giant lizards following you through supermarkets. I suppose Carrie's labels were cautionary, but as with a curious college kid, they had the reverse effect and egged me on.

I couldn't wait to get the Dirty Mojave Mix and the Scary Sonoran Stuff in the ground. Right away, I took out my Mikita jackhammer with a spade bit and broke up some soil to increase its tilth (crumbliness). I combined the seed mixes with Mexican gold poppy seeds, one-quarter-inch-minus decomposed granite, and a little fine composted bark mulch in a galvanized bucket. Carrying the bucket, I walked back and forth in parallel lines, tossing handfuls of the mix into the garden. Then I turned ninety degrees and did the same thing again, then lightly raked in the mix.

Wildflower seeds are intelligent. They wait for just the right conditions to germinate—sometimes a matter of several years. For some seeds, this means getting bounced down a wash and ending up on the moist, shady side of a rock and sitting there until rain comes. If the water isn't there, the seed will just hunker down and wait for more favorable conditions. Some seeds, such as lupine, have such a tough coating that gardeners have to drop them in a pot of water that has been brought to a boil (but removed from the heat) and soak them all night to simulate the moist conditions that trigger germination in the wild.

In addition, wildflowers that bloom in the desert have the good sense to go dormant when they need to, which explains why they are sometimes referred to as ephemerals. Spring ephemerals go dormant before the hot months blow in, while the summer ones wait for the monsoon storms to bring the required warm, moist conditions before they germinate and bloom. Both spring- and summer-blooming wildflowers preserve themselves against harsh conditions by moving into dormancy. Some gardeners view this as a liability, but these adaptations are precisely what make desert wildflowers perfect for arid gardens, and for me, planting ephemeral wildflowers is another great way to add

surprise and mystery to your garden. If you want less surprise, just add more water.

Try as they may, landscapers usually fail miserably at trying to re-create the desert in new subdivisions, and a big part of their failure has to do with a lack of wildflowers. As Verlyn Klinkenborg notes in his book *The Rural Life,* "Landscapers try wherever they can to recreate the silhouette of the desert, the shadow of the heavy limbed saguaros against jagged mountain profiles. The detail is lost, of course..." Unfortunately, Klinkenborg's assessment rings true. Although the popularity of wildflower gardening is slowly catching on, Americans have not yet fully embraced our native annuals. While I admire the efforts of landscapers to save water by using lots of gravel, the result is often sterile and a gross oversimplification of the vegetative patterns of the desert. Yes, the desert is a minimalist landscape, but it is also complex. A sea of gravel punctuated by a couple of cacti doesn't provide enough shade for a lizard, let alone begin to replicate the world of desert plant life. One of the easiest ways to address the problem of too much gravel is with wildflowers. As Carrie says, "Wildflowers knit the landscape together." Ephemeral flowers can bring detail back into a desert yard. They help flesh out and humanize the desert landscape, at least for part of the year.

By far, most of the annual flowers planted in the Southwest (and the entire U.S., for that matter) are not wild. We are hooked on pansies, vincas, and zinnias. For whatever reasons, we cannot turn away from the tarted-up petunias that flow from the Wal-Mart parking-lot garden shop. Like a fat kid heading for a super-sized value meal, we can't stop ourselves from buying traditional annuals. And like super-sized French fries, annual flowers are getting much larger. Sexed-up versions of these plants are continuously being bred to

Firewheel, Goodding's verbena, and silver sage.

have bigger (sometimes freakishly bigger) and "different" colored flowers. Few plants in horticulture have been manipulated more than these.

Even the most casual observer of the annual flower scene will have noticed that the flowers have gotten exceptionally large in recent years. The average pansy bloom, for instance, is easily double the size it used to be, while the diminutive viola blossom has reached the size of the older pansy varieties. The number of colors

The stained-glass effect of evening light on desert marigold and Parry's penstemon.

available has also increased exponentially. You can even buy a black and orange pansy called 'Trick or Treat.'

Traditional annuals are the most chemical- and water-intensive crop a nursery or homeowner can grow. In the nursery, they must be coddled with a cocktail of fungicides and fertilizers in order to make them perfect for the consumer. Besides that, most commercially available annual flowers live only one growing season in Arizona and must be ripped out and replaced twice a year. In most cases, the annuals you buy at Wal-Mart don't reseed, so you are forced to buy more.

Aside from maintenance and ecological concerns, annual flowers have lost their wildness. Many varieties have flowers that nearly eclipse their foliage. Imagine a plant with no visible leaves, just flowers. This might seem almost as good as a grocery bag full of French fries, but perhaps it's too much?

Even master breeders who consult with the world's most prominent pusher of annuals, EuroAmerican, acknowledge that many annuals have become too generic. As Ushio Sakazaki, a world-renowned master breeder who worked for Suntory and now runs his own breeding company, observed: "For all the advances we have made in breeding, we have now reached a point where some varieties are becoming too artificial—and too much alike."

The way Deirdre and I used annuals in our yard would veer radically from traditional annual plantings. We would drive on the wild side of the road. We began by planting seeds from a list of my twenty-one favorite wildflowers; using proven wild annual flowers seemed like a good place to start.

Finding some of these wildflowers has occasionally put me not only on the wild side of the road but potentially on the wrong side of the law. Most of the plants on my list were not too hard to find, but some species were almost impossible to locate at certain times of year. The prairie zinnia, for example, was not for sale through any vendor during one particular early spring. This was frustrating, because it was taunting me with its outrageous floppy gold blossoms in front of public buildings all over Tucson. At the Golf Links Public Library, swaths of it had been planted in the medians all around the parking lot. The prairie zinnia, which spreads from underground rhizomes and can form a solid-gold ground cover, should be easy to grow from root divisions; additionally, taking a root division from a mother plant should not harm the mother plant but rather help it. At least these were some of my rationalizations.

Scott's dryland gardening tools and supplies list

- Mikita HM1500 42-pound electrical jackhammer with spade bit
- 10-pound hickory-handled pick
- Ames fiberglass-handled shovel
- Tierra stainless steel D-handled shovel
- Tierra stainless steel hand trowel
- Corona aluminum hand trowel
- Yum Yum soil conditioner
- Felco #8 Swiss pruners

I figured that with a hand spade and a Styrofoam cup, I could quickly and covertly collect enough for several locations in my yard. I'd hardly be noticed, I surmised, and the remaining plants would be healthier and not as crowded as a result of my divisions. The only problem with this plan was that the Golf Links Public Library, as part of a city cost-cutting plan, shared facilities with the Tucson Police Department. My conundrum was further complicated by the fact that, during this particular winter, the Golf Links Public Library was closed for remodeling, leaving the parking lot empty. I would be an easy target for the TPD if they decided to crack down on wildflower thieves. On the other hand, it would be a lot of fun and make a good story to dig up some rhizomes right under the watchful gaze of Tucson's finest—the gardener's version of sticking it to the man.

I should emphasize that the landscape in front of the Golf Links Library is manmade, not public wild land. The zinnias I was after were planted by landscapers and were not wild plants. I would never steal any plants, especially cactus, from the wild or take a *whole* plant out of any manmade landscape. My prairie zinnia digging would scarcely be noticeable and would actually leave the mother plant intact and possibly re-invigorated. Yes, these are feeble justifications, but they comforted me at the time.

One Sunday morning in January, I made my way down to the library with a stainless steel trowel and a thirty-two-ounce Styrofoam cup. I noted a couple of police cars at the back of the complex and several City of Tucson trucks in the parking lot, but it looked pretty deserted. I had brought along a copy of Rick Bass's book *The Ninemile Wolves* that I had checked out from the library—my alibi in case someone asked what I was up to. I felt a little like a wolf myself, slinking around on a bright, clear Sabbath day doing my best to avoid humans. Driving around the parking lot, I wondered where all the prairie zinnias had gone. A week ago it had seemed as if I was tripping all over them on my way into the library. Then I saw it: a big backhoe, now sitting idle, had been digging up the bed where most of the prairie zinnias had stood; now piles of them lay ripped up and stacked like clumps of sod along a trench. So as it turned out, there was no need for secrecy. These flowers were on their way to the dump, and if I didn't take them, they'd end up in the landfill. With my trusty trowel, I confidently dug up a cupful. As far as I know, no officers of the law even looked my direction.

The prairie zinnia is surprisingly grass-like, and without the flowers, the root system and leaves of the plant look a lot like those of Bermuda grass. This made me wonder if it would be as aggressive as Bermuda. If so, this would be even better for the hot street-side strip where I planted it. I put the rhizomes down into

Brittlebush blooms hover over silver-blue foliage.

the clay dirt and cut most of their tops off so they wouldn't transpire much water while their roots were getting established. Within a couple of weeks, little grass-blade-like foliage was emerging above the soil. These wild plants with a cost of zero pleased me immensely.

Roadside Weeds and Desert Willow Adventures

One scorching June afternoon, I found myself kneeling down on the dusty shoulder of Tucson's busy Valencia Road. I was looking for seeds of a wild plant I had seen blooming in the area earlier in the spring. The plant, prickly poppy (*Argemone platyceras*), was to become the latest addition to my garden. Its distinctive white and yellow fried-egg-colored flowers and bold blue-green foliage were sure to be a spring hit on the wild edges of the garden. This was a coyote of a flower, one that seemed to like the disturbed soil and extra water often found along roadways.

But I was having a hard time finding the prickly poppy, which by June had dried to a tawny brown and become hard to distinguish amongst the grasses. Finally I found the remains of a sprawling poppy near a creosote bush. The prickly seed heads, combined with the rat-a-tat of gunfire from an adjacent shooting range, made me jumpy. Still, after a while I settled into a rhythm, and the seed harvest, even with the gunfire, became a pleasure. I was right in the moment, filling my Ziploc freezer bag full of wild promise. When I got home, I carefully labeled the bag and tossed it into my steel seed bin with a host of other seeds I was saving for fall. I was happy to have these roadside weeds in the kitty.

By roadside weeds, I don't mean invasive exotics such as Russian thistle (tumbleweed) and spurge. I mean plants like spreading fleabane, dogweed, Mexican gold poppy, Parry's penstemon, Arizona lupine, prickly poppy, velvet mesquite, and desert willow (more about desert willows later). The roadside weeds I'm advocating are natives, and although they can be aggressive, they are generally not invasive and will not be changing the ecosystem too much. Compared to the newest Monrovia heavenly bamboo introduction, these plants get relatively little attention from the gardening public. They seem to need an advocate.

Gardening with wild and weedy plants requires relinquishing some control. This is not to say that the plants are in charge, but rather that, from time to time, they have something to say about how the garden evolves. Still, as I sowed my prickly poppy seeds, I did so with a little ambivalence. I had never seen prickly poppies in any garden, not even public botanical gardens. I wondered if my poppies would be so aggressive that they would take over huge portions of the yard. I already had native fleabane spreading in every conceivable niche, but the fleabane was unimposing enough to fit in well with the other plants around it, even if it went everywhere. The large prickly poppy comes well armed with thorns. It would require more work to weed if it became too much of a thug. (I should mention that in general, though, native plants are not invasive. In fact, one of the best reasons to garden with them is that they usually *aren't* thugs.)

Rick Darke, author of *The American Woodland Garden,* says it this way: "Native plants may be better adapted, but what is more important is that they have proved their ability to coexist within the balance of a forest community, something that cannot be said for many exotics." Translated, this means that if you plant native deer grass (*Muhlenbergia rigens*) next to a wash, it won't march all the way up both sides of the watercourse choking out every other plant in its path the way an invasive exotic like fountain grass (*Pennisetum setaceum*) will.

Standing there with my baggie of prickly poppy seeds on an October morning, I felt as though I was about to release a wild coyote in my back yard. More accurately, my situation was akin to raising a coyote pup. Like a coyote, a wild plant in my garden might not turn out to be completely wild. In either case, there was a level of unpredictability that I wouldn't have if I was raising a golden retriever or planting a pansy. With the wild pup and wild poppy, there was a distinct possibility that the family cat might get eaten and the annual flowerbed overtaken. Still, I liked the big fried-egg flowers hovering over the blue-green foliage like flying saucers, and I was willing to take the risks of planting this roadside weed.

As fond as I am of the wild garden and the roadside weed, I know that a garden needs some structure. Yes, even the native garden should be well ordered, although not in the sense of the grand *allées* of the gardens at Versailles. After a 1999 windstorm ransacked Versailles, garden writer Michael Pollan observed in *The Botany of Desire: A Plant's Eye View of the World*, "When I saw the pictures of the wrecked allées, the straight lines scrabbled, the painterly perspectives ruined, it occurred to me that a less emphatically ordered garden would have been better able to withstand the storm's fury and repair itself afterward." Gardens that imitate formal European models are a poor fit and a maintenance nightmare in the arid western U.S. We don't have the water for lush lawns and traditional clipped hedges. The longer I garden here, the more I respect the tenacious beauty of our native Southwest plants.

This is not to say that our native plants can't benefit from a little selective breeding. One Monrovia finishing-school graduate that recently caught my attention is a desert willow that Monrovia has romantically labeled 'Timeless Beauty'. Monrovia—a high-end wholesale nursery whose salespeople walk the rows in navy blue crested blazers and use the phrase "high bred, well fed" to describe their plants—usually steers clear of native plants; when I saw that Monrovia was introducing a new desert willow, I paid attention. The desert willow was about as close to a roadside weed as anything I'd ever seen in Monrovia's catalog.

By any measure, the desert willow is a tough and scrappy tree. Not a true willow, this Sonoran and Chihuahuan Desert native can form a ten- to twenty-foot-high tree in the worst of conditions. For early summer eye candy, nothing beats desert willow flowers. They range from white to pink to burgundy, with bicolored variations, often with yellow-striped throats. Aside from their visual appeal, the flower buds give off a sweet musky odor that is one of the best scents in a desert garden. In a vacant lot near my home, I have watched a seedling turn into a ten-foot-high tree covered in clouds of pale-pink flowers, which I can often smell from more than a block away. This tree has been bulldozed down twice, and I have watched it recover from its roots to surpass its original stature.

The downside to the desert willow is its seedpods. In the winter after it loses its leaves, four- to eight-inch ribbons the color of dried corn husks hang on the tree, and most people consider this unattractive.

Growing different selections of desert willows is nothing new; Southwestern horticulturists have been scouring the washes and riverbeds for desert willows with unusual characteristics (such as unusual size or flower color) for some time. There is a large desert willow on the Texas A&M campus called 'Bubba.' In other western states, we find two burgundy-flowered varieties, 'Dark Storm' and 'Lucretia Hamilton'; a couple of white types—'Hope' and 'White Storm'—and a large pink-flowered variety named after University of Arizona horticulturist Warren Jones. This is not to mention an earlier bi-colored introduction by Monrovia called 'Regal.'

What Monrovia has done to the desert willow most recently has eliminated its most glaring liability: the sterile 'Timeless Beauty' aborts its seedpods. It also has exceptionally large bicolored (pink and burgundy) flowers with yellow throats. Not only that, because it is sterile, this tree keeps producing flowers long after regular desert willows have stopped flowering, trying in vain to produce seed.

To find out the exact origins of this new plant, I called Monrovia, who didn't have the information at hand and had to investigate. They followed up with an obscure e-mail saying that the plant had originated in Bisbee, Arizona, and had been discovered by a horticulturist named Richard Mathews. Attached to the e-mail was a nonfunctional link to an article in the *Bisbee Observer* about the new desert willow.

Since I couldn't get the article through my local library, I had no choice but to pack up Deirdre and drive to Bisbee in an August monsoon storm on a weekend that corresponded with our fourteenth wedding anniversary.

After checking into the Bisbee Grand Hotel in the historic mining district, I made my way down to the little office of the *Bisbee Observer,* which, as it turns out, closes at 1:00 p.m. on Fridays and opens not at all on weekends. Surely the stately old library across from the hotel would have back issues of the local paper? When the librarian told me that they keep only the two most current issues on hand, the dejected look on my face prompted her to ask, "What are you looking for?"

I've always liked librarians, with their stylish glasses and sweaters, and these Bisbee librarians may be the best in their trade. When I told this one about the desert willow I was looking for, she said, "Oh, the original tree is planted in the parking lot by the Copper Queen Hotel. Richard Mathews planted it there. He's deceased, but his wife Susan works at the county library just up the hill. She is probably working today." I could have kissed her.

So I grabbed Deirdre, and we walked up the hill to the library. On the way, we saw the original 'Timeless Beauty' willow, with a shiny black Harley parked under its branches. The special tree was easy to spot because the parking lot was full of regular desert willows that were already out of bloom, but the 'Timeless Beauty' maintained a full complement of pink and burgundy blossoms. Beneath the tree lay a memorial plaque dedicated to Richard Mathews.

We met Susan Mathews, who told us the story of the tree. Her husband, Richard—an avid hiker, gardener, and mason—had combed Cochise County for rare and unusual plants. He came across the 'Timeless Beauty' purely by accident; it was just one of many trees he dug up from the wild (before the time when people paid a lot of attention to plant-protection laws) and transplanted to a Bisbee park. Its unusual characteristics weren't noticed until the following spring.

This news was completely satisfying. The 'Timeless Beauty' desert willow was not some carefully concocted hybrid cooked up in a Monrovia greenhouse; it was a wild plant, a freak of nature from some high desert canyon or highway shoulder near Bisbee. It was neither "high bred" nor "well fed." For all we know, this willow was just a roadside weed until Richard Mathews unceremoniously dug it up and moved it to a Bisbee park.

And really, this is what gardening with roadside weeds is all about. When we begin to see the variations and charms of our local plants, a world of gardening possibilities presents itself. We bring wildness home. We see that we are only marginally in charge of our plants.

As I watch the mighty blue-green leaves of my prickly poppies push out of the ground in the spring, it occurs to me how much power there is in this wild seed. As with a human embryo, a wild seed harbors an element of surprise. Certainly, the new plant will somewhat resemble its parents, but just as likely, it will differ from its relatives in some detail—maybe even a signifi-

Sacred datura flowers.

cant detail like the size of flowers or lack of bean pods in the 'Timeless Beauty' desert willow. There is always a chance for surprise in the wild garden.

The White Desert Garden

Since we planned to spend many morning and evening hours in the front yard, our first inclination was to design and plant a white garden in this area. White flowers show up like little stars at dawn and dusk and seem the perfect complement to an iced tea and an Adirondack chair after a long day at work.

A white garden carries a lot of high-priced European baggage with it. The most renowned pale garden in the world is the White Garden at Vita Sackville-West's Sissinghurst in England. Sissinghurst, now a National Trust garden, is maintained by a crack team of horticulturists. It begins flowering in April with a succession of white tulips and wallflowers and continues into October with Michaelmas daisies and dahlias. In the godforsaken barrens of the Sonoran Desert, the odds of growing nice white tulips are equivalent to a snowball's chances in hell. Designing a garden whose paradigm was a garden halfway across the world in rain-soaked England seems kind of crazy. As far as I can tell from photos (I have not yet had the pleasure of visiting Sissinghurst), precious few, if any, of the flowers in Sissinghurst's White Garden grow well in the Sonoran Desert.

Since we were already in love with the Sonoran flora, it didn't seem like much of a sacrifice to exclude tulips and dahlias from our design. In fact, looking at pictures of Sissinghurst was rather like looking through a reference book of pedigreed dogs, knowing full well that you would end up with a well-groomed coyote.

We began the process of selecting tough and wily white plants for this little crescent. The first plants we put in formed the bones of the garden—the trees. Since we already had the large mesquite, we needed smaller trees. We planted one tenaza, a small tree with fragrant white puffball flowers that smell like vanilla-spiked honey. In several key positions around the crescent, we planted Chihuahuan orchid shrubs (*Bauhinia lunaroides*), which bloomed clouds of small white flowers in spring, followed by orchid-shaped leaves.

Between the trees and shrubs we planted a tough group of native perennials. Goodding's verbena and tufted evening primrose were at the front of the border, and sacred datura sidled up to an ice-blue Weber's agave. The aluminum-white leaves of 'Silver Cloud' Texas ranger made a foil to the lacy foreground of purple moss verbena.

We reserved small areas for special Sonoran plants: a single gray-blue slipper plant that I had spotted growing amongst a thousand regular green slipper plants figured prominently. I also planted the thorny and billowing white Sonoran nightshade, given to me by a friend who was disappointed that it did not flower blue.

Although some of these white-flowering plants were spectacular successes, after two years it was clear that the white garden needed rethinking. The white version of the autumn sage (*Salvia greggii*) that we had planted turned out to be a feeble cousin of the red version and as frail as an invalid. Many of my prized giant snapdragons, always a challenge, had succumbed due to wet

feet. Our principal problem was that the too-heavy soil drained poorly. Many of the white native plants I wanted to grow demanded sharp drainage, and the garden wasn't as interesting as it should be year-round.

We found one other problem with the white garden: it was boring! To many gardeners, calling a white garden—considered the epitome of understatement and refinement—"boring" borders on heresy. In some gardening circles planting hot-colored plants in a white garden is déclassé—like wearing a Sex Pistols T-shirt to a wedding. There is no denying an element of snobbery to the whole idea of white gardens.

I liked the idea of having little bright stars of white flowers to look at in the morning and evening, but I decided I didn't want my plant choices limited by the

Tufted evening primrose flowers.

color white. I would look over the adobe wall and out into the wild landscape of canary yellows, lipstick pinks, and chromium blues, and in comparison the white garden looked like, pardon the simile, a shrinking violet—too restrained and contrived. It needed a closer affinity with the wild garden just outside the wall. It craved color, and I don't mean the artificial color of a bed full of hybrid pansies. I wanted the glowing jewel-like blossoms of penstemons and salvias to turn up the volume in the crescent. This garden wanted to rock, and I was trying to make it waltz.

Dogweed and red wooden chair.

We began again. I moved or discarded all the plants that weren't thriving. I planted two more big blue Weber's agaves to punctuate the crescent. I double-dug the crescent shape and mixed in Yum Yum soil conditioner and bat guano. Yum Yum makes a good soil amendment for alkaline Southwestern soils. It comes packaged in a flour sack and is made in New Mexico by ex-hippies. Next, I replaced white salvia with red-flowered firecracker penstemons and big gold Mt. Lemmon marigolds (*Tagetes lemmonii*), and I put Texas violet sage (*Salvia farinacea*) next to the Sonoran nightshade. This bold new mix seemed more at home here. In the fall, we seeded the whole area with Mexican gold

Work boots, yellow door, soft-tipped agave.

poppy, desert bluebell, and evening-scented stock seeds. By spring the garden was humming with bright-hot desert color. The firecracker penstemons poked up through the Texas violet sage, and hundreds of purple-white native fleabanes formed a crazy carpet under the whole show. It was as loud and dirty as a Keith Richards guitar solo, and it suited me fine.

"Anything but Yellow"

Often derided as gaudy and low-class, yellow has a rep-utation as the trailer trash of garden colors. Maybe because of its high visibility, yellow is not a color many people dare to wear. Honestly, how many yellow shirts do you own? The color of smiley-face stickers and golden arches, yellow is not taken seriously in the gar-dening world; considered shallow, it gets no respect.

Many a newcomer has walked into the Civano Nursery and announced, "I want some flowers, and I don't care what they are as long as they're not yellow." This is what I call the "anything but yellow" syndrome. But all this animosity is misguided in a desert garden. I'm going to assert that yellow is an absolutely essential color in a desert yard; next to yellow, white looks inbred and soft. If you can choose only one color in your desert garden, make it yellow. You'll find more tough yellow flowers in the desert than any other color.

In our garden, we embraced yellow in the front yard. While listening to Cold Play sing, "it was all yel-low," we painted our front door yellow and planted large yellow-striped agaves nearby. I can think of no better complement to the lime green of a palo verde trunk than a bright yellow flower, and some of the first plants to appear beneath our green tree were the tiny yellow daisies of the shrubby dogweed. On the fringes of the property, big silver brittlebushes with their air-borne flowers screamed yellow, with the tenacious desert marigold not far behind.

Yellow is the color of the pure energy of the sun, and in country full of light, it offers the perfect celestial expression, well reflecting the solar culture of the desert.

It took me a while to make my peace with yellow. I flirted with purples, which reside on the opposite side of the color wheel from yellow, but the range of purples is quite limited in desert plants. Part of my problem, I discovered, was that I had harbored a snobbish attitude about yellow.

Most of the garden books I consulted suggested that yellow was all about energy and movement and suggested that the eye could not rest on yellow too long. The texts cautioned so strongly against using yellow as a garden's predominant color that you might believe that looking at too much yellow, like staring into the sun, would burn holes in your retinas. The only place to use yellow, they suggested, was along a corridor you are trying to move people through. I visited a used bookstore and noticed that in a series of garden books, each with a separate garden color as its topic, yellow was the only one in stock. In fact, there were no fewer than six used copies of *The Color Garden (Yellow)* lined up on the shelf. I picked up a copy for the bargain price of three dollars. Poor yellow—it was (pardon the mixed metaphor) the redheaded stepchild of the garden.

I believed a lot of what these texts said and tried to use a little splash of it here and there but not everywhere. Then one day, I stopped resisting, and a world of plants opened up to me. I began to see yellow everywhere in the desert. I also saw that the best complements to yellows in the desert garden were blue grays and silver grays. Fortunately, these seemed to be the color of the foliage on many yellow-flowering desert plants. Also, many of the fine desert succulents, like Parry's agave, were a gray or glaucous blue that made a near-perfect backdrop for a gold or yellow flower.

Not only did we embrace the yellow plant palette in the garden, we brought it into the architecture of our home. We painted all our doors the color of sundrops (*Calylophus hartwegii*). We took that same yellow and painted a horizontal strip of concrete below a single brick step leading to our front door. I painted many zinc-coated pots yellow and left their galvanized rims exposed to match our silver corrugated roof. For all of this I got courage from Derek Jarman's Dungeness cottage, with its gold window casements on black walls.

I began to see the desert world as blue, green, and yellow: the big blue sky, the green palo verde trunk, and the ubiquitous punctuation of yellow flowers. These three colors became our paint palette on the eaves, doors, and windowsills, but the color most people remember about our home and garden is yellow. "You know," they say, "it's the house with the yellow door and desert marigolds."

Best yellow-flowered desert trees

- Berlandier acacia, blue palo verde, catclaw acacia, foothills palo verde, palo blanco, palo brea, sweet acacia, velvet mesquite

Best yellow-flowered desert shrubs and ground covers

- brittlebush, chocolate flower, Cooper's paperflower, damianita daisy, desert marigold, desert milkweed, desert senna, dogweed, Mexican hat, prairie zinnia, shrubby senna, 'Sierra Gold', Sierra sundrops, sundrops, Superstition mallow, turpentine bush, yellow chuparosa

Crêpe-paper-like sundrops blossoms.

Best yellow-flowered desert vines

■ yellow morning glory vine, yellow orchid vine

Best desert agaves and cacti featuring yellow

■ Engelmann's prickly pear, fishhook barrel, golden barrel, Mexican blue barrel, tuxedo spine prickly pear, variegated century plant, white stripe agave, yellow hesperaloe

Curtains of Vines

In the 1920s, Arizonans knew how to keep cool. Before the invention of air conditioning, most homes had sleeping porches, also called Arizona rooms, and many homes used awnings and trellised vines to protect west- and south-facing windows from the intense afternoon sun. On really hot days, these vines would be hosed down for extra cooling. This method was so venerable that Phoenicians called it "the way Cleopatra kept cool," according to Bruce Berger's *The Telling Distance.* Even now, when many Southwesterners would consider living without air conditioning as preposterous as living in a desert without a golf course, it seemed to me that using trellised vines was still a great way to passively cool our house.

A 1989 ASHRAE (the American Society of Heating, Refrigerating, and Air-Conditioning Engineers) study found that windows fully shaded from the outside have a summer solar heat-gain reduction of 80 percent, and this study only considered the value of blocking the solar radiation. It did not consider the second cooling benefit that vines provide: their leaves transpire water. Like a tiny misting system too small to feel but nonetheless effective, vines cool the air by releasing tiny amounts of water vapor. Since many vines grow fifteen

feet or more in one season, they offered us a quick shade fix while our young trees were filling in.

If you think of the plants in your yard as outdoor furniture, vines are the curtains and ceilings of the garden. Vines can divide the yard into "rooms" without the expense and permanence of brick and mortar partitions, and they can provide as much overhead protection from the sun as a covered porch can. Because vines grow vertically, they fit well in even the smallest yards. In spite of all these benefits, vines are still not widely planted in Southwest yards.

Our small yard seemed the perfect candidate to drape with vines. We had little horizontal space but lots of vertical space. As I'll discuss later, we installed two water-harvesting culverts in our back yard that needed some vines to soften their look of gleaming steel. Because the vines I wanted to use required something to climb on, I designed two circular steel trellises to slide over the tops of our culverts. On these round trellises, I planted a pair of yellow morning glory vines (*Merremia aurea*), which are native to southern Baja California and fit in fine with the Mexican theme in our back yard. Their vigorous star-shaped leaves have covered my culverts and turned them into twin green cylinders. In the summer, when the heat really gets cranking, this vine is covered with an astounding number of big, bright yellow morning glory-like flowers. After flowering, the vine produces a papery seedpod that contains up to four seeds. Zoë has taken up collecting the seeds, which look exactly like black velvet-covered rabbit droppings. The seeds are as hard as rocks and are highly sought after among native plant enthusiasts. As evidence of how much they flower, we now have a storage-size freezer bag nearly full of black seed that Zoë gathered from the two plants in just one growing season.

Next to one of the water-harvesting culverts, I built a little ocotillo fence on which I hung my collection of

A desert marigold stem arches across an Engelmann's prickly pear pad.

Southwestern license plates. This fence needed a petite little wisp of a vine to climb up through, but not obscure, the license plates. I chose a vine that I had seen growing out of a crack in the cement at the Arizona-Sonora Desert Museum—a small native called twining snapdragon (*Maurandya antirrhiniflora*). At the Desert Museum, the snapdragon vine was growing up over a little agave in a gauzy halo. This vine sent out a fine embroidery of tiny heart-shaped leaves and a good number of purple and white snapdragon-shaped flowers. I love the way the green tendrils and white flowers look draped across Utah's Delicate Arch license plate, and the purple flowers look particularly fine against the green backdrop of the Colorado plate. This little vine, which rarely reaches ten feet high, was perfect for the ocotillo fence.

Maybe the best thing about the license-plate ocotillo trellis is the way it brought some family history into the garden. The white plate with a blue zia symbol and the letters S.A.B. was originally attached to the front bumper of my Grandpa Calhoun's 1933 Packard Phaeton Touring car. The zia symbol, which is a stylized Native American sun, is found on the New Mexico flag and license plate and has long been ubiquitous in advertising around the Southwest. The letters stood for Southern Arizona Bank, an institution that no longer exists but which evidently produced stylish advertisements with a Southwestern touch. I found this plate, with its three prominent bullet holes, on Grandpa's old ranch in Star Valley near Payson, Arizona. That ranch, with its creaky floorboards, screened sleeping porch, and trickling spring choked with watercress, was the setting for many boyhood adventures. The property was filled with buffalo gourds, piñon pines, manzanitas, and one-seed juniper trees. My father's family sold the ranch ten years ago, and I haven't had the heart to

'Baja Red' queen's wreath climbing our steel ramada.

go back and see what's become of it. I'm told that part of it has been turned into a gated, master-planned golf community, and that's something I'd rather not see. I'd rather just look at my Southern Arizona Bank license plate and think about the wild and beautiful place I used to know, a place where timber rattlesnakes lived in the crawl space and bobcats crept down the hillside to drink from the spring.

Of all the plates in the collection, my favorite is the Utah centennial plate featuring the famous orange Delicate Arch set against a blue background. This seemingly tenuous sandstone formation in Arches National Park still looms large in my imagination as an icon of the high desert and a place of wonder. A road trip to Arches was the first trip that Deirdre and I took together. A couple of young college kids trying to escape the cold of northern Utah, we borrowed the rusted-out 1976 Toyota pickup from Deirdre's dad, threw our mountain bikes in the back, and drove southeast. We pitched our tent by the banks of the Colorado, filled our water bottles from a spring in the cleft of a rock, and rode our bikes on the barely christened Slickrock Trail. We were crazy in love, and our dreams of a life together seemed as big and limitless as the Moab sky. It felt like our future together would always be punctuated by orange spires, red towers, and delicate arches. We ate foil-wrapped dinners with our feet in the sand and watched the Colorado go by. Unlike the current ski-industry-sponsored Utah plate featuring a little skier and the slogan "The Greatest Snow on Earth," Utah's centennial plate celebrated something more deserving and unusual: a desert rock formation. In a state where love of the desert sometimes comes hard, a big, bold Delicate Arch license plate had to be counted as a small victory for those enamored with Utah's arid wild lands.

We have a Colorado plate in our collection that also reminds us of our Western ramblings. When Zoë was a toddler we packed up our little Honda Civic and headed out for Durango, Colorado. We camped in a dense ponderosa pine forest during a rainstorm. Our eventual destination was Santa Fe, which took us through Pagosa Springs, where we stopped and spent the night in a motel with a sulfur-scented hot spring that Zoë couldn't get enough of. With our skin smelling of rotten eggs, we arrived in Santa Fe under a bright sunny sky and ate tacos grilled by street vendors in front of the Governor's Palace. We didn't get our New Mexico plate until years later, when garden photographer Charles Mann sent us one with another zia symbol in its center.

Our old license plates provided a fun way to spice up an old ocotillo trellis. When people see the garden for the first time, it's often what they comment on most. The license plate trellis could be considered a tribute to the Western nomad. If living in the West is about freedom, it's fine with me if our garden suggests travel.

I can think of few things better than a vine that provides both shade and fruit, and that's exactly what the native "stinky" passion vine (*Passiflora foetida*) does. This plant grows very fast, and in a single summer, it nearly smothered our ramada, providing an awning of velvety silver three-lobed leaves overhead. The native passion vine blooms a pale-blue flower followed by excellent fruit about the size of a large grape that falls to the ground when ripe. That first summer, Zoë and I often went outside in the evening to collect the fruit. We found that if we waited until morning the crickets would beat us to it, leaving only hollowed-out husks. You eat the fruit by biting off one end and squeezing the pulp into your mouth, discarding the skin. Its flavor and texture suggest a cross between a grape and a kiwi fruit: it has the juicy, slippery insides of a grape and the little crunchy black seeds of a kiwi. Our vine produced copious amounts of fruit, and we ate loads of it throughout the summer, especially after monsoon storms induced mass blooming and fruiting. When the fruit drop was heavy, Zoë took pockets full of passion fruit to school to share with her friends.

Most people don't plant the passion vine for its fruit. This plant is a big-time butterfly plant and is the primary food source for the gulf fritillary butterfly. Butterfly gardeners are crazy for this plant. Personally, I welcome the gulf fritillary with the same enthusiasm that the Egyptians welcomed the plague of frogs. The butterfly plague begins with the appearance of fuzzy black and copper caterpillars, which you don't notice until you look up and think, "Hmm, this vine looks a little more sparse than it did last week." At this point, the caterpillars are not visible to your untrained eye. Then you notice one happily chewing a pubescent silver leaf. Once you find him, your eye will become attuned, and you will quickly discover all of his brothers and sisters and cousins lunching on every section of your vine. I don't spray any non-organic chemicals in my yard, but I have been tempted to spray BT (*Bacillus thuringiensis israelensis*) to rid my vine of caterpillars. BT is a naturally occurring bacterium so benign that even organic farmers use it. I would have used it myself, but I worried that I would greatly upset my butterfly-gardening peers. After all, the editor of *Butterfly Gardening* magazine lives right around the corner from me, and she would be sure to notice the decrease in fritillary activity the following summer. They are good people, but if I riled them up they might burn me in effigy at their annual meeting. So I held off on the spraying and tried to make my peace with the gulf fritillary.

The larvae ate my native passion vine to the ground, and it didn't come back the next year. Because of its popularity with the local caterpillars, I had just about given up on this particular native plant—until I noticed seedlings popping up in several places around

"Stinky" passion vine in flower.

the ramada. All those fruit casings that Zoë and I had tossed into the garden after sucking out the pulp must have contained a few seeds. It appeared we would have another summer full of passion fruit and shade.

During the time I thought the passion vine was a goner in our garden, I planted another vine I had long admired in its place: 'Baja Red' queen's wreath (*Antigonon leptopus* 'Baja Red'). I had seen this vine in an all-red garden at the Arizona-Sonora Desert Museum, rambling over a rustic ramada made of twisted mesquite logs. Its leaves were big and heart-shaped and crinkled like crinoline, and its sprays of flowers were a deep reddish magenta. Regular queen's wreath is common around the old barrio areas of Tucson and is also fondly known as San Miguelito. I had also seen queen's wreath in its native range in southern Sonora, rambling over trees and shrubs on canyon hillsides. I liked this big-hearted vine right away. It has a feminine appearance and looks like something your granny would plant, but it is tougher than a tomcat. Queen's wreath grows from a big tuberous root, which stores starch and water and allows the plant to survive tough desert conditions.

My neighbor around the corner had queen's wreath planted at the base of his foothills palo verde tree. In the late summer, a cloud of pink flowers would emerge like a hat at the top of his tree. The pink created a wonderful contrast with the lime-green palo verde branches. In our back garden, which was primarily red in color, pink wouldn't work—I needed the reddest flowers we could find, and 'Baja Red' seemed to fit the bill.

A slow starter, it climbed ten or twelve feet the first year. By the second year the queen's wreath and the passion vine were fighting for the entire ramada ceiling. It was like the showdown of the desert climbers. Who would dominate? It turned out that the passion vine

Coke bottle, white stripe agave, Ford pickup, Mexican fencepost cactus, and "big pink pincushion" cactus.

got a jump-start on the queen's wreath, but the queen's wreath engulfed the passion vine later in the season. Queen's wreath does attract a lot of bees, so you might want to be careful if you're allergic to bee stings. However, in my experience, the queen's wreath provides so many flowers that the bees are busy gathering nectar and pollinating and are not concerned with the humans below.

Other un-vinelike vines are vining cacti. Some of them will climb through trees like the tentacles of a giant octopus, and others will crawl along the ground like fat green boa constrictors. Nearly all of them have large white blooms that illuminate the night several times throughout the year.

On the steel ramada in our back yard, we are growing a strange climbing cactus along with passion vine and queen's wreath. It's a large, cantankerous plant called the moon cactus (*Harrisia bonplandii*). I saved this cactus from under a tree that was being cut down; its former owner was ready to put it in the trash. Using green nursery tie-tape, I've woven this climbing cactus in and out of the steel grid of our ramada. One of the moon cactus's charms and frustrations is that, as with the mesquite tree, there is no straight to it. It twists and bends and coils on itself like a garden hose. I am trying to encourage it to grow up, yet it insists on sending out large shoots that swoop down toward the ground. So I tie and trestle the lower branches to promote upward growth. There is one branch growing toward the top of the ramada in exactly the fashion I had imagined, but its fellow branches refuse to follow its lead.

Just when I'm thinking the trash might have been the proper home for this cactus, summer comes. The moon cactus begins to grow strong green arms in all directions. One summer night, we noticed a flower bud the size of a man's fist. The next night that bud exploded into an obscenely large and lusty white flower caked with globs of yellow pollen. When it blooms, it is like its namesake: dogs bark, cars stop, and the neighbors come over. No one can resist a freakishly large moon-like cactus flower.

Our moon cactus blooms next to our recycled mirrored door, which is often framed by its blooms. On one such night, Deirdre and I stayed up late taking pictures. In the digital photos we were shooting, we noticed that, along with the cactus flower, we had included ourselves in the pictures. For fun, we took a self-portrait.

Mexican Fencepost Fences

Perhaps the strangest and most striking cactus and succulent garden in Arizona is tucked away in a corner at the Arizona-Sonora Desert Museum. The garden, which uses a purple wall as a backdrop, holds court beneath a large ironwood tree (pictured on page 96). The weirdest plants in this garden are the eighteen or so six-foot-high totempole cacti (*Pachycereus schottii* var. *monstrosus,* formerly *Lophocereus schottii* var. *monstrosus*) that stand up like avocado-green melting candles against the purple wall. As their common name suggests, they resemble totem poles. As far as I know, this odd shape does not appear elsewhere in nature.

Other fun twists in this garden include a giant octopus of a climbing cactus, draped throughout the limbs of the ironwood. In the shade of the tree, a mass planting of a Baja barrel cactus (*Ferocactus rectispinus*) looks like a five-member punk-rock band with red spiked hair, buried up to their necks. Native to Baja California, Mexico, it has the longest spines of any barrel cactus. Indeed, it resembles a spiked hairdo assembled with super glue. Canyon penstemon and desert marigolds grow among the barrel cacti. Flanking the barrel cacti is a triad of cycads (*Dioon edulis*), strange, low palm-like plants, which add tropical flair to this bizarre and sculptural garden.

In my opinion, this little gem, tucked away between the art gallery and the Ironwood Terraces restaurant, embodies the high art of desert gardening. It has offered great inspiration to me in designing with cactus. I have photographed this vignette of plants many times, and I use one of these photos as my computer screensaver to remind me how elegant and diverse a mixed planting of cacti, trees, and wildflowers can be. This garden and others like it have motivated me to attempt innovations with cacti and succulents in my own garden.

I began my own cactus strangeness by taking a plant I love—the fire barrel (*Ferocactus pringlei*)—and using it in a nontraditional way, as address numbers atop a wall. I should explain. I wanted to bring the candy-apple red spines of this lovely cactus up onto the top of our adobe wall. Per city regulations, we also needed to post our address numbers on our home. So we decided to kill two birds with one stone. I found five little zinc-dipped pots that matched our galvanized roof. We painted the lower portions of the pots to match the purple-blue trim of our house, and I insulated them with a spray-in foam (after all, it's going to get hot sitting in a metal pot on top of a wall, even for a cactus). Deirdre carefully painted on our address numbers, because, just as in many aspects of our marriage, she is better at the details. Finally, we selected five of the reddest fire barrels we could find, which had been carefully chosen by local cactus grower John Weeks for their bright coloration, and planted them in a good-quality cactus mix. After a monsoon storm, these fire barrels fairly glow red. They are one of my favorite plants to photograph after rain.

Along the wall below these pots lay a hot little strip of dirt between the street and the wall. Since it was only two feet wide, we needed vertical plants there. We settled on an old Mexican idea, making a fence outside

Portrait of Scott and Deirdre with moon cactus, June 2004.

the fence with Mexican fencepost cacti (*Pachycereus marginatus*). Cactus fences are an old practice dating back at least to the early part of the sixteenth century. Used as barriers for people and cattle, cactus fences are common today in Mexico, Peru, Chile, and Argentina. Various cacti are used in fencing, including Indian fig, Argentine toothpick, cholla, and Peruvian apple cactus. Such fences are green and lush and secure. So why don't we build more living cactus fences here in the Southwest? Who wouldn't be pleased with a big, bold green fence that never needs painting and is not subject to the height restrictions typically imposed on fences in newer subdivisions?

For my purposes, I know of no finer fence-type cactus than the standard Mexican fencepost. These columnar plants with their five sides and white-striped spines are some of the most attractive upright cactus for home landscapes. They are part of the essence of Mexican gardens and have a cameo appearance in the film *Frida*—a Mexican fencepost fence surrounds Diego Rivera and Frida Kahlo's Mexico City studio. When Zoë was no more than six years old, we were watching a documentary that showed giant multi-armed saguaro cacti being bulldozed to make way for development; Zoë cried inconsolably. There is something about columnar cacti that people respond to; I think it's because they remind us of ourselves—two arms, a torso, a neck, and a rounded head.

The only problem with planting a Mexican fencepost fence is, as with the palo blanco trees we planted, they are not reliably cold-hardy on the chilliest nights in our part of Tucson. What we had going for us was a south-facing wall with lots of surface to radiate heat back to the cactus at night. Also, the blacktop less than two feet away would hold in heat after dark. Even in this favorable microclimate, we are consistently five degrees colder than Tucson International Airport at night. This meant that we needed a backup plan to keep the cactus warm some nights. I knew that I could place Styrofoam cups over the growing tips of our cactus, so I went down to the local Magpies Gourmet Pizza and got twenty large (thirty-two-ounce) cups. During the first few freezes of the year, I placed the cups over the growing tips of my cacti—not stylish, but functional. (What we really wanted was a Mexican fencepost stocking cap, preferably in red.)

I also have a great passion for prickly pear cacti. As landscape plants they are about as trouble-free as it gets. Truly a New World plant, prickly pear has species native to every state west of Nebraska. Surprisingly, the prickly pear is rare in U.S. horticulture. Nothing compares with the prickly pear's Mickey Mouse-eared form. Its bold green, blue-green, or purple ovals make the perfect foil for many fine-textured Western native plants. Here, arranged from large to small, are a few species with ornamental (and culinary) significance.

Indian fig prickly pear (*Opuntia ficus-indica*) The pads of the Indian fig, or *nopal,* one of the oldest species in horticulture, are cut into strips called *nopalitos,* cooked, and used in Mexican dishes, and the fruit is sold in open-air Mexican markets. When sautéed, nopalitos make a fine addition to omelets. They taste a little like green beans. Besides their nutritional value, which is significant, the *Opuntia ficus-indica* makes a fine, hulking landscape specimen. When used for landscaping, the Indian fig can be planted as a large hedge or living fence or shaped to form a sort of tree. Although native to the Americas, it has been cultivated in Spain, Italy, and North Africa for hundreds of years. Its long history in Mediterranean Europe has even led to the belief, especially among Sicilians, that the Indian fig is a native Sicilian plant. In the desert Southwest, the nearly spineless Indian fig is favored above all other prickly pears by javelinas. Several of the finest specimens in my front yard were eaten to the ground by these desert "pigs," and my only remaining specimen is nicely fenced in the bed on the north patio.

Dinner plate or **clockface prickly pear** (*Opuntia robusta*) The freakishly large round pads of this prickly pear make it an excellent candidate for an accent plant in a garden. The yellow fruits are sweeter than the more common Engelmann's prickly pear fruits. A good substitute for Indian fig where wild pigs are a problem, dinner plate prickly pears replaced my pig-eaten plants in the front yard. The enormous pads draw frequent remarks. Because the dinner plate becomes such a huge specimen, it's advisable to stack large rocks around its base to support it in windstorms. In our garden we used little cairns of riprap to keep the dinner plates nicely above the ground.

Fire barrel cactus on adobe wall.

Santa Rita prickly pear (*Opuntia violacea santa-rita*) Shortly after we moved back to Tucson, Deirdre and I were driving around the rolling hills of the Tucson Mountains one early winter day in her old VW Cabriolet convertible. We came upon a house with an entire yard of Santa Rita prickly pear. The hundreds of plants created an arresting sea of purple inter-mingled with lime-green palo verde trunks. It was a Dr. Seuss-style landscape, but to us it looked awfully good, even appropriate, in the shadow of the rocky Tucson Mountains.

Because of its unusual purple color, the Santa Rita prickly pear is often the first cactus that newcomers to the desert choose for their yards. Its distinctive pads, which are often spade shaped, turn deep purple in winter and blue-gray with purple edges in summer. There

Santa Rita prickly pear in full bud.

is much variation in the pad shape and color, so choose your specimen carefully. I like the way the Santa Rita prickly pear looks when planted with damianita daisy (*Chrysactinia mexicana*) and Goodding's verbena.

Engelmann's prickly pear (*Opuntia engelmannii*) This is the classic prickly pear of Arizona. Its magenta fruit and juice have inspired many a Southwestern chef, and it is the only prickly pear whose juice is commercially available. I inherited three large Engelmann's on the common area in front of my house. These three plants have produced enough fruit to keep our fridge well-stocked with prickly pear juice for lemonade and other cheap luxuries (more on this in a bit).

Tuxedo spine prickly pear (*Opuntia violacea* var. *macrocentra*) The black and white spines of this diminutive purple prickly pear give it its common name. A fine garden specimen, it is relatively cold-hardy and features bi-colored yellow and orange flowers. It looks particularly fine when planted amidst moss verbena and desert marigold, as in my front garden.

Beavertail prickly pear (*Opuntia basilaris*) Less than a foot high, the beavertail has glaucous pads shaped somewhat like its namesake's. One of the most cold-hardy of the prickly pears, its native range extends up to an elevation of six thousand feet. Its small size and magenta blooms make it one of the most manageable and beautiful of the ornamental prickly pears. This is a great plant for Utah, Colorado, and New Mexico gardens, where less hardy prickly pears would freeze out.

Plants along our Mexican fencepost fence garden

- desert bluebells, dogweed, firecracker penstemon, Mexican fencepost cactus, Parry's penstemon, superb penstemon, sweet acacia, twisted-leaf yucca

Prickly Pear Pleasures

Since growing apples in most of the low desert is doomed to failure, prickly pears make a nice—but totally different—substitute. Our interest in prickly pear cooking began after finding bushels of Engelmann's prickly pear fruit going to waste in a vacant lot behind our apartment complex in central Tucson.

Prickly pear product suppliers

Cheri's Desert Harvest
800-743-1141 (Tucson, Arizona)
www.cherisdesertharvest.com
Cheri's Desert Harvest offers a selection of prickly pear jellies and syrups. Call or order from website.

Arizona Cactus Ranch
520-625-4419, 800-582-9903 (Green Valley, Arizona)
www.arizonacactusranch.com
Unsweetened prickly pear nectar, jam, and other products. Call or order from website.

Chef Alan Zeman's Southwestern Originals
520-886-1745 (Tucson, Arizona)
www.fuegorestaurant.com
Prickly Pear Barbecue Glaze, Sonoran Seasoning, and other products. Call for order form, or order from website.

Rivenrock Gardens
Nipomo, California, www.rivenrock.com
Organically grown, nearly spineless prickly pear pads in several grades. Picked fresh the day they are shipped and worth the price. Order from website. Also carries ornamental landscape cactus.

Armed with an old newspaper recipe for cactus jelly and a pair of taco tongs, Deirdre and I gently separated the purple fruit from the blue-green pads. On that blisteringly hot August afternoon, we picked our first bucket of cactus pears, or *tunas*.

After processing the fruit into juice, I drank my first sip. Fresh prickly pear juice has a gossamer magenta color, and its color and taste are deep and mysterious, like a cross between cranberries and watermelon rind. It is not bitter, but not sweet.

Fruit processing

When Engelmann's prickly pear fruit is ripe, it will turn a deep red color and will separate easily from the pad. Do not try to pick the fruit or handle it with your fingers, but use tongs and a five-gallon bucket. Wash the fruit and blend it in a sturdy food processor. Strain the juice through a colander lined with four layers of cheesecloth. The cheesecloth will strain out any of the remaining glochids left in the pulp and juice mixture. Let juice strain for 20–30 minutes. Discard pulp, seeds, and cheesecloth, taking care not to drop pulp or seeds into the juice. Freeze the magenta-colored juice in ice-cube trays for later use, or use fresh.

That first year, we put up jars of prickly pear jelly and prickly pear pancake syrup. Later, we found other uses for prickly pear nectar: mixed into lemonade, whipped into sorbets and salad dressings, used as a glaze for pork loin, and—perhaps its best and highest use—as the main ingredient in the prickly pear margarita.

I teach an annual class on prickly pear cooking, and it never fails that sometime during the class I will be asked about stickers. I make it clear that I've been stuck in my ankles, calves, stomach, and wrists. I've pulled stickers from my forearms, shoulders, chest, and neck. I've even had cactus spines in my buttocks several times. For the purposes of the class, I make an important and reassuring point: I've never had a cactus spine, sticker, or glochid (tiny hair-like stickers) in my mouth, gums, or intestinal tract.

Totempole cactus, ironwood tree, canyon penstemon, and Baja "punk rock hairdo" barrel cactus, Arizona-Sonora Desert Museum.

Recipes

PRICKLY PEAR LEMONADE

4 cups water

juice of 6 lemons, seeded but not strained

½ cup prickly pear juice (or 3–4 frozen prickly pear ice cubes)

⅔ cup sugar

1 sliced lemon

Combine water, lemon juice, prickly pear juice, and sugar. Stir until sugar dissolves. Add lemon slices. Serve over ice or chill until cold.

MAKES 5 SERVINGS.

NUCLEAR SUNSET PRICKLY PEAR MARGARITAS

¼ cup lemon juice

¼ cup lime juice

½ cup high-quality tequila

⅓ cup prickly pear juice

⅓ cup sugar

¼ cup triple sec

1 cup cold water

1 tablespoon orange zest

Stir together lemon and lime juices, tequila, prickly pear juice, sugar, triple sec, and cold water until sugar dissolves. Serve over ice. Garnish with orange zest.

MAKES 2 SERVINGS (ABOUT 8 OUNCES EACH).

PRICKLY PEAR JELLY

(Adapted from a recipe in *The Arizona Daily Star*)

4 cups prickly pear juice

4 tablespoons fresh lemon juice

4 teaspoons Pomona's Universal Pectin

2 cups sugar

4 teaspoons calcium water (included with Pomona's Universal Pectin)

Boil clean jelly jars and lids for ten minutes.

In a saucepan, bring prickly pear juice and lemon juice to a full boil. Mix the pectin and 1 cup of the sugar together.

When the juice reaches a full boil, add the pectin and sugar mixture. Remove from heat and mix with a wire whisk. Return to heat. Add second cup of sugar and bring back to boil while stirring. Remove from heat.

Add calcium water while stirring and mix well.

Using tongs, remove jars from boiling water bath and drain briefly on clean dish towel.

Turn jars right-side up and fill with hot syrup to within ½ inch of lip. Wipe each lip carefully with a clean damp cloth, then fish lids out of the boiling water with tongs and set one on each jar. Using a dish towel to hold the jars, screw down the lids with rings. Set filled jars in water bath and boil for 8 minutes. Remove and invert briefly. Cool on rack.

Make sure lids pop down before storing in a cool, dark place.

MAKES 3 JARS (12 OUNCES EACH).

save water

save water— making the most of drought and deluge

Desert cultures have always taken extravagant measures to bring water to gardens.

As early as 5500 B.C., gardeners in Egypt and Mesopotamia cut channels into the banks of the Nile and Euphrates Rivers to irrigate plants. According to some accounts, watering the Hanging Gardens of Babylon required teams of men to haul water from the river around the clock.

A Brief History of Desert Water

In the Sonoran Desert, ancient Native Americans now known as the Hohokam diverted the cool Salt River into more than five hundred miles of canals to water

Candelilla growing from a ceramic water-spitting frog (opposite); bat-faced cuphea (inset); Sierra sundrops and dogweed (pages 98–99).

the fertile valley in the area where Phoenix now sits. From A.D. 350 to 1450, the Hohokam grew crops of maize, beans, squash, and melons. As the territory was settled by Anglo-Americans, the abandoned Hohokam canals caught the attention of an enterprising ex-Confederate soldier, Jack Swilling, who hatched a plan to take water from the Salt via canal once again, to grow crops to sell to area miners. In 1867 Swilling began what became a modern canal system that now fingers across Phoenix. Beginning with the dedication of Roosevelt Dam in 1911, the U.S. government started a series of massive reclamation projects that dammed the Salt River in four places, providing Phoenix with reliable year-round water. By the 1940s and 50s, most Salt River water was used for mining, cotton, and citrus. But another use was gaining prominence: irrigating Bermuda grass lawns. The water that would bubble up to flood-irrigate my grandmother's grass and citrus trees had traveled in some of the same channels that the Hohokam carved.

When Salt River water alone was not enough to slake the thirst of central Arizona's booming metro areas, Arizonans embarked on the most improbable water project of all: the Central Arizona Project, or CAP. Planned since the 1940s and completed in 1993 at a cost of over $4 billion, the CAP consists of a 336-mile-long system of aqueducts, tunnels, pumping plants, and pipelines that carries Colorado River water from Lake Havasu near Parker, Arizona, to the southern boundary of the San Xavier Indian Reservation fourteen miles southwest of Tucson.

But the history of water here also shows what little thought was given to conservation until very recently. Water in Arizona was mostly viewed from a supply-side point of view. Although Lake Powell (at the border of Arizona and Utah) has been drawn down to low water levels it hasn't seen since it was first filled, and some experts have predicted that Arizona may lose its CAP allocation of Colorado River water in the next ten years, most politicians won't even acknowledge that when it comes to water use we are writing postdated checks we can't cash. The history of water projects in Arizona seems to prove the old saying: "What direction does water flow in Arizona? Uphill toward money." And the great rushing of water toward money has not gone unnoticed by your average consumer. As a long-time Mesa resident once told me, "I've always thought it was my job to use as much water as I could so at least the golf courses won't get it all."

Even nationally, water shortages have begun to affect lots of folks in the nursery business. I have followed a hot debate within the American National Landscape Association (ANLA) over the way member nurseries should address drought issues. Should members fight to preserve the watering status quo, or should they change the way they do business to promote drought-tolerant plantings and efficient irrigation techniques? From what I can see, the main thrust of the ANLA's policy toward drought has been to publicly endorse drought-tolerant planting and irrigation techniques while fighting restrictions on watering behind the scenes. This position seems to recognize the recalcitrance of the public to change its habits.

In the arid West, we know a lot about how hard it is to get people to change their landscaping habits, but it hasn't stopped us from trying. In my view, our main job as Southwest horticulturalists is to help our customers come up with innovative and beautiful solutions to drought. This is possible; even Laura Bush has a rainwater cistern and a garden full of Texas-native plants. Our own governor, Janet Napolitano, has begun to address the Southwest's water realities. In a radio interview in July of 2004, she advocated that Arizonans create a "culture of [water] conservation." Although she provided no details about how this would happen, it seemed like the best idea I'd heard out of a politician in a long time. If people begin to think that saving water in their landscapes is part of being an Arizonan, that would go a long way toward creating beautiful low-water-use landscapes with a real desert sense of place.

The story of the watercress-choked spring that my family sold with our ranch illustrates the direction of flowing water in Arizona. When I did a little research on what had become of our family's old homestead, I found out that it was sold to a development company not so much for the land, most of which remains undeveloped, but rather for its high-quality spring and water rights. As it turns out, the spring has been piped

Mexican hairy barrel, "elegant Oaxacan pincushion" cactus, and slipper plant.

into a new community, which, in the tradition of many Arizona communities, is named after the plants that were destroyed to create it. Chaparral Pines, or Chappy Pines as some of the Payson locals call it, has become a flash point for water issues. With its large homes and extensive golf course, Chappy Pines is one of the only green spots in Payson, which has had severe water restrictions in place for several years on account of persistent drought. Some locals are upset that the Chappy Pines golf course remains a verdant emerald-green while their own back yards are gravel with a struggling juniper that they can only water on certain days each week. Mostly, the locals are upset that the City of Payson did not buy our family's old spring for the municipal water supply. The most troubling aspect for me is that the spring and surrounding vegetation are probably gone. Where are the watercress and coyote willows?

My brothers and I would scan that stream for hours in search of minnows. My uncle Donald, who was then living on the ranch full-time, constructed a cowboy Jacuzzi out of local rock. He pumped water from the spring into his newly constructed circular stone tub and let the overflow run into the apple orchard. At the end of a hot day he would lounge in the cold water with a turkey leg in one hand like royalty; Uncle Donald was fond of cooking turkey in a subterranean pit, an experience I was destined to repeat. That was the only time we could remember that there was a half-decent apple crop.

When my dad took us to the ranch, all the normal rules of civilization were suspended. On the drive up the Beeline Highway, our flatulent springer spaniel, Rufus, would snore and fart on the floorboards. When we got to the ranch, Rufus would sleep on the beds in the bunkhouse with us. Dad would begin to relax. After a few days at the ranch combing the hills for arrowheads and knocking tin cans off a fence with a .22-caliber Remington rifle, none of us wanted to go home. We played cards at night, ate pie from a local diner, and cooked breakfast on a woodstove that blackened the ceiling with smoke. There was no hot water, and the cold water that gurgled out of the kitchen spigot came right from the spring. On arriving at the ranch, my dad made a tradition of opening the creaky screen door to the kitchen and walking directly to the sink; he would put his mouth over the faucet and drink right from the tap, something we knew for sure would be prohibited at home. He would smile and say, "Boys, that's good water." Even then, we suspected, but didn't know exactly, just how sweet and precious that spring water was.

My Experience with Desert Water

Growing up in metropolitan Phoenix in the 1970s and 80s gave me a warped view of water in the desert. At the northern edge of the hottest American desert, our front yard was planted with Bermuda grass, mulberry trees, and two large grapefruit trees. My brothers and I mowed, edged, and watered the lawn. By today's standards, the lawn was large, and we spent many a Saturday morning behind the mower. In winter, we overseeded the lawn with rye, so there was no seasonal relief from mowing. Keeping the lawn well cut was a priority at our home, and my father oversaw its maintenance with a keen eye, although mowing the lawn was about the only time we actually spent *on* it. The task of mowing taught me pride in a job well done; it also taught me to hate watering and mowing that cursed lawn.

It was easy to forget we were living in a desert. When I had my own garden, I vowed to find ways to conserve water and to think differently about what a yard could be.

I had read about Beth Chatto's gravel garden in the driest corner of England, which thrives on an average of only twenty inches of annual rainfall without any supplemental irrigation. The idea of not installing irrigation appealed to me. It would save me time, money, and labor. However, I was living in a city that averaged only eleven inches of rain per year and could easily go sixty consecutive days with daytime high temperatures over 100 degrees. I had seen a few desert gardens that survived without supplemental irrigation. They consisted almost solely of cacti. I love cacti and wanted a sizable number of them in my garden, but did I want a garden composed entirely of cacti? My answer was no. I knew that I wanted a mixed arrangement of desert perennials, cacti, and agaves that looked "garden quality." In Tucson this would require supplemental irrigation.

The one climate factor that most defines the desert is lack of rainfall. As the cliché goes, "It's a dry heat." Rainfall is scant, and evapotranspiration rates are high. Evapotranspiration (ET) is the amount of water that a plant sweats out of pores in its leaves, combined with the amount of water that evaporates from the soil surface. In Tucson the average ET is seventy-seven inches a year and average rainfall eleven inches a year. In Phoenix, the annual ET is eighty inches on average, with an average of ten inches yearly rain. This means that Tucson has a 7:1 ratio between water that is evapotranspired and water available from rainfall; in Phoenix the ratio is 8:1. Farmers and gardeners soon learn that only natives and a few desert-adapted plants can survive on ten or eleven inches of annual rainfall. Even many drought-tolerant native plants require supplemental irrigation, especially as they are getting established. In some respects, I was just like the Hohokam. I had a little patch of desert that needed irrigation.

I was going to take extravagant measures to bring water to my garden. I would not build a masonry dam or a cement-lined canal; the water I needed was right over my head. Without my lifting a finger, my sombrero of a corrugated metal roof would shed around 14,000 gallons of pure rainwater annually. I began to believe that my house was like a mountain. Rain would fall on its peaks and slopes and run down to the lowlands, where I would store it in tanks and in the ground. I was like the owner of a small water company with control over a tiny watershed. All I had to do was figure out a way to contain and store the waters flowing from the mountain.

After some research, I learned that there are two methods of harvesting rainwater: simple and complex. The simple method involves contouring your land so that rainwater flows into holding areas that can be used by adjacent plants. Holding areas are often made by constructing crescent-shaped soil berms that trap water as it flows downhill. These berms are sometimes called boomerangs.

Simple methods of rainwater harvesting can include patios, sidewalks, or driveways that slope toward a planting area or tree. These simple methods direct and slow the water down, allowing it to percolate into the soil. Complex rainwater-harvesting methods involve capturing the water in above- or below-ground cisterns. The most successful systems use a combination of simple and complex methods, based on the realities of a garden's layout. We figured we could use some simple methods on the front garden and complex methods in back.

I decided to make my complex system as simple as possible. To do this, I would place my culvert above ground. By storing rainwater above ground, I would not need pumps or other moving parts to transfer it to my plants; I could let gravity do the work. Naturally it turned out, as it often does, that just because a system is simple doesn't mean it's easy to install.

While driving through one of Tucson's historic barrios, we spotted some corrugated steel culverts being used to hold rainwater. The culverts were upended

into a cement slab. Each 3-foot-wide by 8-foot-high culvert would hold 480 gallons of rainwater. I determined that to catch most of the water that would cascade from our gutters, I would need two culverts for the main house and one larger culvert for the guest-house roof and deck.

The 16-gauge steel culverts looked a bit like gleaming jet fuselages, and at first we had some question as to whether they would work aesthetically in the garden. But since Tucson is the home of the largest airplane graveyard in the nation, what could be more apropos than a garden accessory that looked like an airplane part? In the end we decided that the corrugated zinc-coated spirals had enough in common with our corrugated sombrero roof to fit in stylistically.

I gathered my friends, and over two weekends of wielding picks and shovels, we excavated three holes for our culverts. The holes were a foot deep and four feet wide. After we finished digging, we placed bricks in the bottom of the holes and set a sheet of concrete-reinforcing mesh on the bricks. Using wheelbarrows and fifty bags of concrete (sixty pounds each), we mixed enough cement to pour an 8-inch slab for each culvert. After pouring each slab, we carefully upended its culvert into the wet cement and made adjustments with 2 × 4 bracing to make sure each culvert was plumb.

If there was a grand gesture in our garden, the rainwater culverts were it. Not only did their gleaming spiral tops peek up over the wall, the custom rain gutters we installed extended beyond the roofline. When it rained, dramatic twin waterfalls poured into the culverts.

I liked the way the culverts looked; they added an industrial/ranch edge to the garden. But being a plant person, I wanted to incorporate them more into the living part of the garden and help them appear slightly more organic. As I mentioned earlier, I covered the culverts with my favorite Sonoran Desert vine, yellow morning glory.

The culverts were efficient at harvesting water. I calculated how much water I could collect from my roof, based on the capacity of my culverts, then derived the approximate water needs of each of my plants. I made the following chart:

Month	Average monthy rainfall (inches)	Amount collected off 1,500-sq.-ft. roof (gallons)	Amount needed for irrigation (gallons)	Surplus or deficit
January	1.2	1,073	300	773
February	1.0	825	450	375
March	.9	743	890	−147
April	.3	243	890	−647
May	.3	248	1,040	−792
June	0	0	1,040	−1,040
July	1.3	1,073	1,040	33
August	1.8	1,485	1,040	445
September	1.0	825	890	−65
October	.7	578	740	−162
November	.7	578	450	128
December	1.4	1,155	300	855
Total	12	8,826	9,070	−244

After making this chart, I realized that if we had a below-average rainfall year or planted more plants (both of which seemed likely), I would need to supplement my watering system with the city's potable water. Even in an average year, I would end up at least 244 gallons short. So I created a dual plumbing system using ball valves and backflow prevention valves that allowed me to turn on rainwater when I had it and

The graceful curve of sharkskin agave hybrid leaves.

potable water when the culverts ran dry.

As it happened, all three years following the initial planting of my garden were drought years—some of the worst to date in Arizona history. This meant that I would use more city water than expected. In fact, that first year I used a good amount of it to get my numerous new plants established. Comparing my water bill with those of my Civano neighbors who were using secondary water to irrigate showed that, aside from a couple of people with pools and lawns, my potable water use was on the upper end of the scale. That alarmed me a little the first couple of years, but as my plants settled in and the rains came, I knew my reliance on city water would decrease.

By the second year the yellow morning glory vine had grown high and thick around the circular culverts. Deirdre had attached several steel dragonflies to the trellis, and the culverts were starting to look at home in the garden. The plants in the rear garden were beginning to come into their own and seemed to love the rainwater. For large chunks of time in fall 2003 and spring 2004 my garden was watered by nothing but good, clean rainwater from my gleaming jet fuselages.

In February of 2004, a big Pacific storm lingered over Arizona, and for the first time since 2001 our yearly rainfall total was above average. In anticipation of the storm, I had emptied our culverts by giving all my trees a deep watering. During winter rains, I had to watch the weather carefully to avoid major overflowing. The winter rains came at a time when my plants needed little water, but at times I would water anyway to make capacity for an incoming storm, and this time I was ready for a whopper. Having rainwater culverts made wet weather more interesting. Should I drain the culverts and make more capacity, or sit tight? Usually when I drained the culverts, it was almost a guarantee that the storm would not live up to its billing, but during this February storm, I had planned it just right. A

gentle rain tapped on my roof all night, and just before it tapered off at 7:00 a.m., I heard the spigot sound of the culverts overflowing.

All of this monitoring the culverts, obsession with weather, and recording of rainfall totals caused Deirdre and Zoë to give me a new name. During a slumber party Zoë held at our home, I stepped out on the porch to watch some monsoon rain come down. I could be still as a pillar when watching rainfall, and I suppose I lost track of time. When I turned around to go into the house, nine giggling girls had their faces pressed to the windows, making fun of me. Deirdre and Zoë announced that my Native American name should be "Rainwatcher." Come to think of it, it was a pretty good name for me—Rainwatcher it is.

Before I could use all the water we collected in February, a big March storm dropped another inch and a half of rain. The rain lasted two days. Our culverts overflowed into the street. I was so excited that it was hard to sleep during the storm, and the sound of rain on our tin roof didn't help.

The day after the storm, Zoë and I were driving to the B & B Cactus Farm to pick up some Mexican blue barrel cacti. Not far from home, we got stopped at the Tanque Verde Creek, which was running too high to drive across. Since we were in no hurry, we got out to look at the wonderful muddy water. Zoë waded in the shallows while big cotton-candy clouds floated over the snow-capped Rincon Mountains.

During summer storms, when the rains were less predictable and more violent, I would go out in my boxer shorts in the middle of the night to check the water level (a habit Deirdre considers mildly disturbing). Even under troubled skies, a shiny circle of silver filled to the brim with clean, clear rainwater is a sight that I never tire of seeing, even if it means going out in my underwear. In these summer storms, the culverts might fill up in fifteen minutes, with overflow running down the street like a river.

Being the CEO of my own little water company was tricky and interesting business; I became supremely aware that there were many factors beyond my control. It gave me a lot of respect for the plants that could hang onto dear life between the rains. Those tough plants were an integral part of my rainwater harvesting system; without them any semblance of a garden would not be practical without conspicuous and probably foolish water use. Foolish water use was a Western tradition, but one I aimed to avoid. Could I be extravagant and not foolish? It was hard to say, but as an extravagant miser I channeled my water and planted my plants like a modern-day Hohokam. I hoped the rains—and my garden—would not disappear.

When I analyzed our 2003 water bills in order to enter our yard in a Xeriscape contest sponsored by the Arizona Department of Water Resources and a local botanical garden, I discovered that we were doing pretty well in our efforts to save water and create a micro-Eden. I had worried that my unbridled inclusion of desert plants might have somewhat undermined our water conservation goals. Through a "Memorandum of Understanding" with the City, our conservation-minded community of Civano had agreed to use less than fifty-three gallons of potable water per person per day. I'm not sure what the breakdown is between potable and other water but, includ-

Say goodbye to cheap water

If there's one thing that might keep folks from turning the Southwest into the Midwest, it will be expensive water. For those of us pushing for more desert-adapted landscapes, word of higher water rates is almost good news. The fact that states like Utah, which have had some of the lowest water rates in the nation, are considering new progressive-use water rates (the more you use, the more expensive the water becomes), can only be considered a positive sign. At some point, this is going to be more than an issue of watering lawns but, rather, of how we develop in the Southwest. With Lake Powell at only 42 percent of capacity, some federal officials say that if the drought persists for one or two more years, the great body of water behind Glen Canyon Dam could dry up as early as 2007.

This chart, from a 2001 report, *Utah's Water Resources: Planning for the Future*, shows that with the exception of a few forward-thinking cities, Western water is less expensive than the national average and probably a lot cheaper than it should be. Compare the water rates per 1,000 gallons in these Western cities:

Reno, NV	$3.39
Los Angeles, CA	$2.22
Park City, UT	$2.20
Tucson, AZ	$1.81
Las Vegas, NV	$1.65
Phoenix, AZ	$1.61
Albuquerque, NM	$1.41
Denver, CO	$1.14
Salt Lake City, UT	$0.87
Provo, UT	$0.75
Sacramento, CA	$0.75
AVERAGE	$1.63
National Average	$1.96

ing reclaimed water—which most Civano residents used for landscape watering—the community averaged a total of eighty-two gallons per person per day.

Since our house never hooked up to the reclaimed water, I can't say how our potable-water use compares with that of our neighbors; for both indoor and outdoor water use, our family's average potable water use was fifty gallons per person per day. To put that in perspective, the average Tucsonan uses 134 gallons per day compared with your average Utah resident, who used a whopping 321 gallons per day in 2001. Because of my prodigious gardening activities outside, without rainwater there was small chance of our meeting the fifty-three gallon per person per day goal. Rainwater meant the difference between a minimal landscape and a minimally extravagant garden. The extra fourteen hundred gallons of rainwater we captured and released several times throughout the year left us feeling a little less encumbered by regulations; because of it, we felt a little more free to design and plant the yard.

Fifty gallons each and every day seemed like plenty. When you think about it, it's almost like we each had a fifty-five-gallon drum of water to use as we pleased each day. For our family, it turned out to be just enough.

The Ungardened Garden—Saving Water with Gravel, Brick, and Stone

In the American Southwest, I began a lifelong love affair with a pile of rock.

—Edward Abbey,
A Voice Crying in the Wilderness: Notes from a Secret Journal

One Saturday morning we were eating breakfast outside. We had the windows open and were playing the Lucinda Williams album *Car Wheels on a Gravel Road* on the stereo inside. The title cut reminded me of gardens, or rather the different feeling you get when you're in a garden—especially a garden with some gravel paths. The sound of crunching gravel evokes images of a more rural and slower-paced America. One of our nursery customers calls her rock mulch "yellow crunch," which sounds to me like the name of a breakfast cereal, but it accurately describes the sound of walking on gravel. There is nothing like the crunch of decomposed granite underfoot to signal that you have left the industrial world of parking lots and shopping malls and stepped into a desert garden.

When I drive to a remote area to go hiking, the sensation of pulling off the asphalt and onto a dirt road signals my body to relax. My breathing slows and my blood pressure decreases. I roll down the windows. The mind and body know you are getting close to the wild and healing natural world. This is how we should feel when we enter a garden.

Regardless of the materials you use, making a patio or pathway instead of a planting bed saves water. In desert gardens—and as a plant lover this is hard for me to say—you can't put plants everywhere and save water unless all you're planting is cacti. But by designating some areas as patios, with oasis areas around where you live, and larger fringe areas as transition and xeric zones, you can say you have a lush desert garden without that sounding like an oxymoron.

In the dry zone, keeping your plants separated by a little bare ground will also conserve water. When you walk in the desert, you'll notice that the plants are spaced farther apart than in other ecosystems. As Bruce Berger says in his book *The Telling Distance,* "The most telling emptiness lies between living things. For the desert plant, exiled by thirst, catching water with its roots, exposed on all sides, in competition with its own kind, emptiness is the very source of life."

I'm not suggesting that our gardens should be great

The back yard, with its twin cisterns, in the early spring.

expanses of gravel punctuated with two or three cacti. In many new subdivisions, we see too few plants and too much gravel; without plants, a stark sea of gravel can make the desert garden a fiery hell of reflected heat in the summer. I am reminded of a recent trip I took down Interstate 215 in Las Vegas. This newly constructed freeway's embankments consisted of miles and miles of rock without a single plant on either side of the road. On one hand, the design saved water, but the harsh ribbons of glaring rock were pretty hard to take.

At noon, the Mexican checkerboard is dappled with pop bottle shadows.

Sunglasses were a necessity.

When we thought about the surfaces for our garden paths and patios, we knew they had to be permeable. Water had to be able to get into the soil. Beyond that, paving materials should have some relationship to the materials used on the house or the theme of the garden. On our front patio, we used brick, set in sand, that matched the bricks we used on our windowsills. The curvilinear patio echoed the curve of the low adobe wall that surrounded it. The brick patio sloped toward our planted areas to take advantage of the rain that fell on it. In a light rain, the water would soak into the

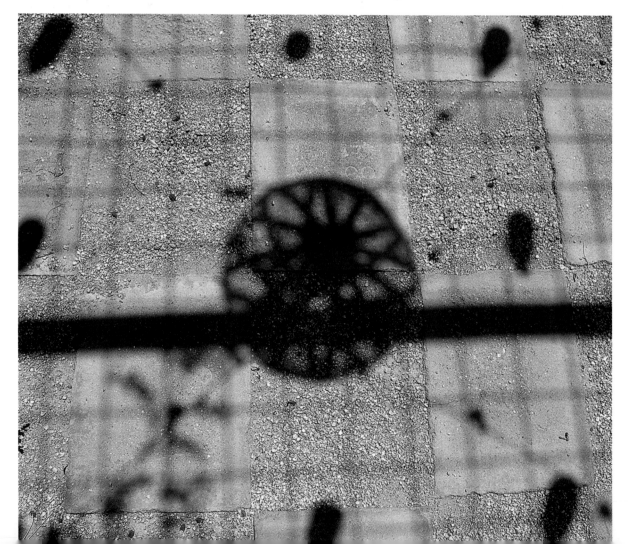

cracks between the bricks and water the surrounding beds. In heavy rain the water would run off in sheets towards the same beds. Considering that we cooked, ate, read, and slept on the patio, the brick was a good, durable surface for this high-traffic area. In the back yard, with its steel ramada festooned with Mexican pop bottles and its riot of red Sonoran plants, we opted for a solution a bit more out of the ordinary.

We had been keeping an eye on a pile of fired Sasabe adobe bricks that had been abandoned on pallets on the fringe of our development. They were big, sixty-pound orange rectangles with "Mexico" stamped right in their middles, left over from a big round public building in the center of our community. From my time in the adobe business, I knew that fired adobe was not the most durable material for paving and that over time they would wick up water and begin to flake apart. Still, we couldn't stop thinking about the big orange blocks going unused. Some friends of ours, who shall remain unnamed, had already pilfered a handful of these bricks and made a checkerboard surface in their garden. Pragmatists (cheapskates) that we are, as soon as Deirdre and I saw this, we knew it would work in our yard. I am not ashamed to admit that we borrowed the idea wholesale. We called it our Mexican checkerboard and began to plan our installation.

Since we would be using many, if not all, of these fired bricks, we thought it best to get the blessing of the developer. With permission from the site supervisor, we began loading the bricks into the back of my beat-up Volkswagen Eurovan, twenty or so at a time. As we took the bricks off the pallets, we exposed pack rat middens filled with cholla cactus segments and aluminum-foil burrito wrappers, which gave Deirdre a good reason to let me do more of the lifting. Just moving the bricks was hard work, but our anticipation of the finished patio gave us strength.

We set the adobe in decomposed granite and filled up the cells between the bricks with the same. It was exciting laying out this checkerboard, and the finished effect pleased us more than we had hoped for. The adobe bricks turned a beautiful rich brown after a rain, and in the late summer our red queen's wreath blossoms fell on the checkerboard in charming patterns. It combined the crunchy feel of gravel with the solid feel of brick.

The Mexican checkerboard also slowed down the water that fell on it, letting rain percolate deep into the soil. By default, the empty cells that we had filled with gravel became a little array of French drains. It would have to rain long and hard before the soil in the back yard would be saturated enough for water to run off into the street. The only downside to this patio was that we occasionally tracked gravel into the house on wet days. Deirdre also has a Swiss compunction to sweep the gravel off the top of the adobe block to keep it looking tidy.

On the path to our front door, I cleared an hourglass-shaped swath of dirt for what I hoped would be a wide, generous approach to our house, replacing a smaller path reminiscent of a hiking trail. The hiking-trail path had seemed a little stingy, and I had not prepared and leveled the ground well enough to make it smooth and even. Also, you would have to do a little jig to avoid cacti and agaves that I had planted too close to the path. We wanted a walkway big enough for a couple carrying big, unstable platters of enchiladas to walk side by side without fear of accident. We love enchiladas, and if someone is bringing them to us, it is critical that they have a wide berth on the way to the front door. The enchilada bearer's safety is an important concern.

We raked and leveled the path to the front door until it was ready for gravel. The gravel we purchased was a brownish-red rock called Apache Brown that matched the public pathway in front of our house. Our goal was to integrate our own path with the public one to create a seamless route to our front door. After raking and leveling the brown rock, we wet it down with a hose and rolled it with a water-filled drum. This compacted the rock to make a solid walking surface. Because the path was slightly raised, I dry-set some brown and black riprap rock as a border to stabilize the edges. The rough riprap fit the character of the front garden well. It reminded me of Civilian Conservation Corps projects built in the 1930s in our national parks and monuments. Our front path looked like a Forest

A Topo Crico brand bottle, part of Zoë's Mexican pop bottle collection, at twilight.

Service path to a picnic area, and that suited us fine.

As for harvesting water, the raised paths performed well. At the point where our new path intersected the public path, we formed a small swale (a berm that acts as a small dam to slow down rain water). Water that flowed off our roof would pool and rapidly soak into the surrounding soil. This extra water near the paths caused a profusion of penstemons and globemallows to prosper there. It was the old roadside-wildflower effect. Just as the extra runoff beside a highway creates great wildflower habitat, the planted areas adjacent to my raised pathways were densely vegetated with opportunistic flowers. My raised pathways were just small-scale highways.

During a violent August monsoon thunderstorm in the summer of 2002, I ventured out in the garden in my standard monsoon attire: shorts and Teva river sandals. I wanted to see how the water was flowing through the yard. In the back garden, all of my cisterns were overflowing. I sloshed down our street, which had become an eight- to ten-inch-deep river. Down the block, in a re-created mesquite bosque that serves double duty as a retention basin, the water was over three feet deep and rising. I circled back to my front pathway. On either side of the raised paths, pools of rainwater were percolating deep down into the soil. Soon, I imagined, Arizona poppies would be pushing their way up. By week's end we could have bright orange poppies with red centers beneath our palo verde. The silvery light, punctuated with lightning reflecting off the standing water in the front garden, created a surreal scene: this desert world of water.

By morning the water was gone. It had soaked into the soil. I cooked an egg for breakfast and ate it sitting on the front porch. The air was full of the sharp, clean smell of creosote bush—the desert smelled like rain.

'Baja Red' queen's wreath creeps across the steel ramada while the Mexican disco ball sparkles in the midday light.

living in the yard

living in the yard— cooking, sleeping, and going to the movies

If you've read this far, you've probably already surmised that our front and back yards are not normal.

That is, the front yard is not a big green lawn with a couple of trees, where a real estate agent might stick a sign and few others would venture. We wanted to turn the notion of a front yard on its head. Instead of a highly manicured area that no one used, we wanted to return front-yard living to the front yard. By design, our front door faced onto a gravel hiking path filled with wild trees, shrubs, and flowers. Within this area we aimed to enjoy many a barbecue, movie, and sleep-out.

In our back yard, we wanted to transform a rectangle of beaten earth, hard-up on the street, into a vine-covered, intimate hideaway, a sanctuary for plants, butterflies, hummingbirds—and people. A little quiet place enclosed by a big adobe wall.

Living in the Back Yard

Once we began living in our finished house, the lack of privacy from the street was a little shocking. The house stood there like a naked face, two big eyes with a long nose, looking out on the street. People driving by could look directly into our bedroom. Potential homebuyers would park on the street and

Adobe wall surrounds the northeast patio (opposite); Parry's penstemon (pages 116-117 and inset).

walk right up to the door, thinking that our home was a model, sometimes catching Deirdre in a towel on her way to the shower. We knew we wanted to enclose this space. In a nod to the character of the house, we used mud adobe brick to build a circular wall. I got the idea from a garden at the Arizona-Sonora Desert Museum in which a badly eroded mud adobe wall enclosed a circular planting bed filled with red-flowered Texas betony (*Stachys coccinea*) and salvias. This garden was always alive with hummingbirds, and walking around it felt like exploring a ruin. We wanted a little of that mystery in this back yard.

Without a doubt, the back yard is the most intimate space in our landscape. Flanked by rainwater-harvesting culverts and enclosed by a mud-adobe wall, this 40 × 16-foot garden is Deirdre's personal retreat.

Although the soil and growing conditions were better in the back yard, it still presented considerable horticultural and marital hurdles. The realities of the back yard were as follows:

- The yard faces south, making it the warmest microclimate on the entire lot. This left us with the opportunity to plant some southern Sonoran Desert plants that would be nipped back or killed by frost in other locations on the property.
- With an unnatural longing, Deirdre wanted a water feature.
- The space was divided into thirds by a steel gazebo, leaving no space for large trees.
- Because of its small size, vines and vertical gardening would be critical to the yard's success.
- The whole area was framed and watered by two rainwater-collection culverts, which each hold 422 gallons of water. These would provide irrigation for the plants within the courtyard. Like it or not, these give a strong vertical emphasis to this garden.

Some of the most high-spirited fights of our marriage have been over design issues in gardens. In one Oscar Madison-Felix Unger spat we agreed that Deirdre would get to design the back yard, and I would design the front yard and patios. This was the gardening equivalent of taping a line down the middle of the house. I can't say that it has worked out very well, since we both have infringed on each other's territory considerably.

Deirdre had a notion to plant citrus and pomegranates in this back garden, which ran contrary to my desire to plant cacti and vines from Baja California, Mexico. We reached a compromise in which we planted a 'Wonderful' pomegranate tree in one corner and a variety of Sonoran Desert plants in the rest of the yard.

We also agreed that the garden would have a red theme. We both love the color red and how it looks with the sage green and pale blue trim on our house. The fact that red attracts hummingbirds was also a plus.

Since the pomegranate would be the only non-native tree in our garden, I wondered if it would stick out like a sore thumb. To my surprise, after I selected a nice five-gallon specimen, it seemed right at home in our landscape—perhaps because its red blossoms matched the red theme of the garden.

Although the pomegranate is not native, it has a long history of cultivation in desert regions and is often mentioned in ancient literature. This tree was present in Mesopotamia and in biblical times. The unique shape of the pomegranate, a symbol of fertility, was often depicted in Egyptian jewelry, and pomegranates were placed in King Tut's tomb to sustain him in the next world. In the sexiest book of the Bible, *The Song of Solomon,* the pomegranate figures prominently as a tree to make love under and as a fruit that recalls both temples and the breasts of a woman; "Thy plants are an orchard of pomegranates, with pleasant fruits," says the biblical poet. In Chinese culture, whole pomegranates were rolled onto the floor of the wedding chamber to promote fruitfulness during the consummation of the marriage. Even if you're a guy who can easily disregard ancient Chinese wisdom, what straight male gardener can resist a plant with fruit that recalls the shape of a woman's breasts? Besides its mammary resemblance, the pomegranate is a true desert tree and will survive on only fourteen inches of rain a year. The pomegranate is also one of the rare desert plants with real fall color—its leaves turn an arresting yellow in autumn.

As it turned out, we planted our pomegranate on the verge of an American pomegranate renaissance. In December 2003, a *Time* magazine story touted the culinary and newly realized health benefits of the fruit. At a healthy fast-food outlet in Phoenix, I drank my first bottle of pomegranate juice, produced by a company called Pomwonderful. My mother had often sprinkled the multifaceted, ruby-like pomegranate seeds on fruit salads at Thanksgiving and Christmas, but I had never considered juicing the fruit. The juice had the sweet-tart overtones of cranberry and cherry juice, and the packaging was at least as alluring as the juice itself. It came in a stylish double-globed glass bottle that appeared to have been fashioned within the confines of a push-up bra. Not only was the packaging sexy, Pomwonderful's marketing campaign was equally seductive. Because of pomegranate juice's high antioxidant content—which Pomwonderful claims is higher than that of red wine, blueberries, green tea, and a host of other heart-friendly foods—Pomwonderful used the slogan "Cheat Death" in their print ads.

Against all logic and my strident objections, Deirdre wanted a fountain against the back wall. I knew this would require several weekends of fooling around with electricity and masonry. I also knew that because my wife was strong-willed and generally smarter than me, I would probably end up building a fountain. After I gave up trying to dissuade her, we began to search for small fountain fixtures. We found a painted Mexican frog planter that we modified. When this frog was properly plumbed (we ran a tube from his drain hole to his mouth), water bubbled from the amphibian's mouth. For some reason, the crazy little frog started to grow on me. Maybe his spiral eyes hypnotized me.

To my surprise, Deirdre built the rest of the fountain herself, using spare lumber and a sheet of

Red flowers lead to alluring pomegranate fruit.

galvanized steel. She even used my worm-drive Skil saw for the first time, without incident. Behind the fountain, I installed three old doors we found at a local salvage yard. The center door had a mirror that we lined up with the centerline of our house as a gesture to remedy the feng-shui chi leakage problem mentioned previously. The mirror seemed to do a fine job of reflecting chi back into the house. I could sit at the head of the dinner table with a direct view of the mirror and garden. I could almost feel the chi rushing down the hallway, bouncing off the mirror, and hitting me in the forehead. I believe, although I can't be sure, that the two red and blue Corona beer trays flanking the mirror also helped to contain any stray chi that was bopping around.

I've never been one to spend lots of time fooling around with plants that grow in ponds. I frankly don't understand a plant that will grow by just dangling its roots into water. But Deirdre found some plants called water lettuce that float on the water and multiply like rabbits. At the rate these water lettuce heads propagate themselves, they may shortly be declared an invasive weed by the State of Arizona, as has already happened to water hyacinths and duckweed. But the water lettuce does look pretty good, spreading the color chartreuse out across the surface of the water. There are also a few good native water plants, and I found one that I really liked: yerba mansa (*Anemopsis californica*), which likes boggy conditions. It was a good plant to put in front of the mirrored door in some half-submerged pots in the fountain. Yerba mansa's zinc-oxide-white flowers look stunning emerging from the still waters and reflecting in the mirror. The shape of the yerba mansa flower suggests both prairie coneflower and Mexican hat.

One of the great things about screening is that dividing up an outdoor space usually makes it appear larger than it is. This became readily apparent in my back garden. Before we enclosed the space, the 16 × 40-foot rectangle seemed perfect for a shuffleboard court or horseshoe pit. But after we built our adobe wall, the space seemed plenty big for chairs and a table, trellises and vines, and a small fountain.

The dominant feature in this garden is a steel grid ramada; 'Baja Red' queen's wreath and native passion vine weave their way through the steel squares of the four corner posts and top of the ramada, which are all made of the same metal grid. Also climbing up the ramada is the vining moon cactus.

On trips to Mexico with Zoë, we had accumulated a galvanized bucket full of Mexican pop bottles that now sat idle in the garage. We had moved them from our apartment to our house, but had not found the proper venue for their display. If not for Zoë's protests, they would have been thrown out. Meanwhile, every

White yerba mansa flowers under hybrid mesquite trees (below); Gregg's mist flower (opposite).

Bottle-cap centipede with "stinky" passion vine.

time we went to Mexico, Zoë always seemed to find a new bottle to add to her collection. I could see why Zoë liked them. The Mexican Squirt bottle, for the *toronja* (grapefruit) flavored drink, has a swirling green glass base like a soft-serve ice cream cone. The Crush bottle is fluted and looks like a mini Art Deco skyscraper. Of course we had the classic Mexican Coca-Cola bottles, but there were other obscure brands like Vita, Sidral Mundet, and Topo Crico—remnants of a slower time when people had time to buy a soda at the corner market, drink it on the premises, and return the bottle for a cash deposit. The bottles reminded us of happy journeys into Mexico, where sometimes we had

slowed down enough to eat street tacos and linger over a soda for a good long while in a Colonial plaza. Finally, we used baling wire to hang all twenty-five pop bottles from the ceiling of the ramada and threaded clear Christmas lights among them to add to the market-festival effect. On a trip to Obregón, Sonora, Deirdre purchased a large disco ball made from strips of tin cans that we hung in the center and stuffed full of lights.

Draped with vines and festooned with Mexican soda pop bottles, the steel ramada reminded me of a stall in an outdoor Mexican market, or at least an idealized American vision of a Mexican market. Dangling in the breeze, the Mexican pop bottles became a symbol for our back yard; we began to call it the "Mexican pop bottle" garden.

Continuing the pop-bottle theme, we affixed a bottle-cap centipede to the side of the ramada, along with some magnetized tin-can cockroaches and grasshoppers. Deirdre made magnetic bottle-cap flowers that she arranged on the sheet metal panel of the fountain. The yard was becoming more and more idiosyncratic. We wondered if our neighbors would think it was the work of crackpots. On the contrary, we got a lot of compliments on the Mexican pop-bottle arrangement, none of which included the word "unique." If you stood back a little in the evening and squinted at the bottles glowing in the sunset, you might wonder exactly where in Sonora you were.

We found that hummingbirds were attracted to the pop bottles with red-painted labels. So as not to discourage them, we added a real hummingbird feeder. I'm generally not a big fan of hummingbird feeders. I'd rather let real red flowers do all the work, and it took a while to find a feeder that really fit with the theme of the garden. Most were functional but too plastic; others were decorated with shining glass beads and chimes that recalled a New Age head shop in Sedona. They just weren't the right style for our Mexican pop-bottle garden. Finally, I found some hand-blown bubbled-glass feeders from Mexico, with elegant red glass flowers as the spigots for the hummers' beaks. Their octagonal shape was modeled after French perfume containers of the early 1900s, and the feeders looked so chic, I didn't

A tin-can cockroach at sunset.

care if a hummingbird ever visited. The feeders came in clusters of three, and we hung one directly in front of the mirrored door. This ensured that hummingbird battles over territory could be viewed from both inside and outside the house.

The perennial plant palette had a big emphasis on red plants, with bat-faced cuphea clustered around the palo blanco trees; and firecracker penstemon, slipper plant, and red fire barrel cacti along the wall. We used some blues, like Gregg's mist flower (*Conoclinium greggii,* also known by its folk-medicinal name, boneset) and sundrops to set off the reds.

The back garden was best in late summer following monsoon storms. During and after summer rains, the garden responded as if on steroids. In the sultry heat, it transformed itself into a thick, lush southern Sonoran hideaway. A garden that struts its stuff in summer is an oddity in southern Arizona. Our winter visitors (a.k.a. snowbirds) demand winter-blooming exotics and generally ignore much of the summer-blooming flora. For me, summer is the best time to enjoy the garden. Warm nights filled with night-blooming cacti, yellow morning glory flowers, and burgeoning bat-faced cuphea under the lacy tops of palo blancos make summers in our garden full of magic.

Hair-like Mexican feather grass.

Screaming yellow Sierra sundrops.

Our back-garden trees

- palo blanco, sweet acacia, 'Wonderful' pomegranate

Our back-garden shrubs

- chuparosa, Southwest coral bean

Our back-garden cacti and other succulents

- candelilla, fire barrel, moon cactus, octopus agave, Queen Victoria agave, sharkskin agave hybrid, slipper plant

Our back-garden perennials, wildflowers, and grasses

- bat-faced cuphea, Gregg's mist flower, cherry sage, dogweed, firecracker penstemon, Sierra sundrops, Mexican feather grass

Our back-garden vines

- Arizona grape ivy, 'Baja Red' queen's wreath, "stinky" passion vine, twining snapdragon, yellow morning glory vine

Living in the Front Yard

The front yard has two distinct areas: one public, one private. The public area includes a walking path through our common area, which in turn links with a path to our front door; this is my favorite place to garden. This front area, of which only a portion is technically mine, is the only part of the garden that recalls the New Testament scripture "Consider the lilies of the field, how they grow; they toil not, neither do they spin." This was not to say that I don't have to go out and deadhead flowers, prune, and so on, but that in spring the flowers come like magic, and the path to our front door becomes magical.

The Common Path Planting

Along the common path, I wanted a scene from nature, like turning a corner in a rocky canyon and finding a mesquite tree surrounded by lupine, desert marigold, and fairy duster. I wanted the area to resemble the most beautiful natural area you could imagine coming upon. When we began, it had a barren feel to it with only a palo verde tree and a few small shrubs. We had to get creative.

I began the wildflowering of the areas adjacent to the path by erecting two small fences made from dead ocotillo branches. I had harvested these branches from plants that customers would attempt to return to the nursery. Using a folding pruning saw and baling wire, I easily cobbled together a simple design that, with the exception of the thorny ocotillo branches, looked for all the world like an English willow fence. Maybe it was a subconscious nod to Derek Jarman, who I thought

might build a fence like this if he were still alive and gardening in Arizona. My design included a top rail, a bottom rail, and an X in the center. I made one fence that followed the curve of our adobe wall and one that followed the curve of the path beneath the palo verde tree. I envisioned penstemons shooting up and around these fences and creating hazy, painterly drifts of glaucous stems and flowers.

As I secured the last cane to my new English-style ocotillo fence, I began to consider a shrine for our yard. A Tucson garden without a shrine is like a supermarket parking lot without a taco truck—something is missing. Driving around the south and west sides of Tucson, I had seen front-yard shrines by the dozen. They were mostly vaulted masonry fixtures lit up by Christmas lights and candles and decorated with shiny Virgins of Guadalupe, photos of loved ones, and paper flowers. My favorite Tucson shrine, El Tiradito, is dedicated to a sinner and inconspicuously located behind El Minuto Mexican Restaurant's parking lot downtown. The shrine consists of a crumbling U-shaped adobe wall that is streaked black with candle smoke. Over time, the shrine has evolved into, among other things, a place for mothers to light candles for wayward daughters, and on spring and summer evenings, one sees *many* women lighting candles. I really like El Tiradito's aura of mystery. It evokes ruins and superstitions.

Our front yard was probably too new for ruins and superstitions, but that didn't stop us from making a shrine. Since I've already disclosed my uneasy relationship with the Mormon Church, it's probably no surprise that I built a shrine in my yard dedicated to dirt. The Mormons have never been big on religious statuary, and I remembered Sunday school lessons that cautioned against the worship of graven images, so I decided that a shrine to dirt, while vaguely pagan, would at least not

Neon-pink Parry's penstemon electrifies the edges of the pathways to our front door.

appear overtly Catholic. It would be less offensive to my Mormon friends and family than a collection of twenty or thirty brightly colored Virgin Marys.

Besides the avoidance of religious imagery, dirt seemed a worthy candidate for a shrine. Even considering the uncompromising patches of cement-like caliche, compacted clay, and rock in the soil, I loved my dirt. I had battled it with pick, shovel, and Mikita

Shovel, 8-gauge electrical wiring, ocotillo fence.

jackhammer. Under the summer sun I had cursed the dirt as my pick sparked off the rocky clay. No gardener in his or her right mind would call my dirt "soil." It was just dirt. The dirt was like a good, hard woman in an old marriage. It reminded me of the Lyle Lovett song "She's no lady, she's my wife." That damn dirt had brought forth an exceptional crop of penstemon and supported hosts of beloved desert plants. Once broken up, it drained slowly, but it drained. I'd had that dirt under my nails, in my hair and boots, and mixed with the sweat on the back of my neck. The clay stained my socks orange. After a day of planting in this dirt, I felt like I was part of it, and it didn't feel bad.

All in all, it was a white man's shrine, but I hoped it would still be provocative if not a little funny. I began making the shrine by setting an ocotillo fence in an S-curve between our house and our neighbors'. Onto the fence I lashed an assortment of dull-headed shovels and rakes with cracked handles and missing tines. The tools came from the garden center, where shovels wear out on a regular basis. It seemed appropriate, in this tribute to dirt, to place steel implements that had been defeated by dirt. Between the rakes and shovels I attached four yellow pots containing four torch cacti. On each pot, I painted a letter, spelling out: D-I-R-T.

Inside the Wall, the Private Front

The chief asset of the front side of the house was shade from the ferocious sun, provided by the bright green umbrella of the Chilean mesquite growing just beyond our property line. Because of the afternoon shade and the already good-sized mesquite tree, we were going to ask a lot from this area of the garden. We figured that making an outdoor room was the cheapest way to add square footage to our little bungalow without adding real walls or an actual roof. In addition to gardening, we would cook, eat, sleep, read, and watch movies in this space—a tall request of an *interior* room, let alone an outdoor one.

At first glance, the little 20 × 30-foot patch of dirt didn't seem up to the challenge. Although the small L-shaped area on the northeast side of the house was protected from the afternoon sun, the soil was rock-hard, and I had to "till" it with my favorite desert gardener's tool, the Mikita 42-pound electric jackhammer. I ran into several bands of chalk-white caliche, which I swore fiercely at as I wielded the Mikita against them. I would *conquer* this soil; my plants would thrive here.

My next task was to provide some enclosure. On the north, the area slopes down into a revegetated natural area with a footpath running through it. On the east side of this garden area lies a gravel parking lot that our neighbors and their guests share.

To screen the parking lot, we built a 40-inch-high adobe wall around the area in the shape of a modified question mark. The wall would block our view of the parking lot but allow us to include views of the mountains as part of our garden. Made from Tucson dirt, the wall reflected the architecture of the house (also made from adobe). It also divided the garden into two parts: the wilder section outside the wall and a clearly defined outdoor room inside it.

Within the adobe question mark we built a curvilinear brick patio with the same bricks we used on the windowsills in our house.

Cooking, Eating, and Just Sitting Outside

A couple of weeks after we moved into our house and long before we had any semblance of a garden, we ate Thanksgiving dinner on the north patio, which was not a patio at all but a patch of beaten dirt. Deirdre brought out folding tables, covered them with linen

Our outdoor living room, dining room, bedroom, garden, and movie theater.

tablecloths, and put a pot of white and blue violas on each table. My parents, brothers, and sisters would be here, so we had to keep up appearances.

In the back yard, I had another project—cooking our turkey in a pit. With the jackhammer, I excavated a hole big enough for a twenty-five-pound bird. My friend Eric Clark gave me a bunch of mesquite firewood that I piled into the hole and lit at 3:00 in the morning to get the coals ready so the turkey would be cooked by lunchtime. My fire was impressive. So impressive, in fact, that the leaping flames in close proximity to the eaves of the house made me too nervous and excited to sleep. I sat upright in bed looking out the window at the fire until the flames died down. Then, using clean bedsheets and damp burlap bags, we swaddled the turkey, placed it on a bed of hot rocks, and buried it with southern Arizona dirt. About six hours later, we unearthed the bird and removed the burlap and cotton sheets. For a moment, I worried that the turkey had not cooked—its flesh was as pale as an albino. But I checked the bird's temperature and it was indeed done, maybe even overdone. We carved the turkey with a fork and a butter knife. The meat fell off the bone, and its flavor hinted at mesquite smoke. It made for one of the best Thanksgivings we could remember, and we ate it on a patch of beaten dirt. It got us fired up about cooking outdoors.

You can cook outside just about every month of the year in southern Arizona. Early Spanish, Mexican, and Anglo settlers, as well as Native Americans, often had separate outdoor kitchens in order to avoid heating up their dwellings in the summer. Although we didn't have the space for an outdoor kitchen, we have made do with a rolling barbecue from Sears and a $50 table from Target that we painted to match the house. Although cheap, both have served a couple of kids on a budget pretty well. We've cooked Chilean flank steak, garlic shrimp, and pork tacos with good results. At night, we might set up a light on the dining table after dinner and play Boggle while listening to Billy Bragg sing a Woody Guthrie song:

> They hang like grapes on vines that shine
> And warm the lover's glass like friendly wine
> So, I'd give this world
> Just to dream a dream with you
> On our bed of California stars…

Before we even began building our house, I began building garden furniture. In order to spend any time at all outside, you need a decent place to sit. I saw an article in *Sunset* magazine for something called the Sunset chair and was immediately enchanted. Its design recalled an Adirondack chair, only much more pared down and simple. Somehow the design just felt Western; this Sunset seating looked a lot more like Moab, Utah, than Kennebunkport, Maine. The bad news was that I'd have to build them myself. I sent away for the plans. When I showed the plans to my carpenter friend Duane, he decided that we should build them in the parking lot of our apartment building one Saturday. So we got out the Rolling Stones and started ripping the myriad pieces of half-inch redwood that would become our Sunset chairs. It was a lot of work, and it took us a whole weekend to make two chairs—and this didn't include painting them. We painted the finished Sunset Adirondacks purple-lilac—the same color we later painted our eaves. They sat smartly on our north patio and became a fine place to eat breakfast. To this day, I can't look at those chairs without thinking of the Stones' "Wild Horses" and feeling a little bit proud of myself. I still love the design.

To keep my potted cacti in order, I ordered some wooden shelves called Austrian flower stairs, a name that couldn't sound any further removed from the

Sunset chairs and totem pole cactus in the evening light.

strange and prickly plants I would arrange upon them. I liked the flower stairs' simple design and that they held a lot of pots. Once again, I painted them a purple-lilac. I was getting tired of painting, but I had planted Mexican gold poppy seeds in the pots of the cacti collection and thought the gold poppies would look great with a purple-lilac backdrop.

Finally, in order to avoid more painting, we found cheap brushed-aluminum café chairs to go around our $50 Target table. We found them at IKEA in San Diego and piled our little car full of them for the seven-hour drive back across the burning desert to Tucson. They have proven to be not only shiny and aluminum, but comfortable and low-maintenance as well.

Garden Cinema

On a warm July evening, we had our first outdoor movie night, which let Zoë enjoy being out in the garden without working in it. For her, working in the garden was somewhere just below going to the dentist on the fun scale. Movie night was a great way to get our friends together to enjoy the outdoors and each other's company. If the movie was good, it also kept the kids relatively contained.

In preparation for movie night, we moved our futon out onto the patio and set out a chips and fresh salsa buffet. We invited the neighbors over, and the kids rolled out sleeping bags on the brick pavers while the adults reclined on the futon and assorted furniture. A small alcove in the garage wall makes a perfect spot to stand up a movie screen.

Not a traditional garden activity, watching movies outside has become easy using new technology. The equipment that made our movie night possible included a digital projector, DVD player, and a pair of computer speakers and subwoofer.

A sunset showing of *Greenfingers.*

The first movie we screened in the garden was *That Thing You Do!*—written and directed by Tom Hanks with music by the fabulously gifted band Fountains of Wayne. It's the story of a small-town rock and roll band, the Wonders, who record a song that makes it big. The movie tagline ("In every life there comes a time when that dream you dream becomes that thing you do") doesn't really describe the movie at all, but it seemed to portray the process of dreaming about and building our garden. It was strange to sit outside in a place that had only existed in our minds a few months earlier. During that premiere, monsoon storms threatened, and winds blew in thick moist air, and we narrowly avoided rain.

Later in the summer, we followed up with *Greenfingers,* which as far as I'm concerned is the best gardening movie ever made. We lit up the night with images of green English gardens under a sky of milky stars. *Greenfingers* is based on the true story of English prison inmates who take up gardening and attract the attention of a flamboyant gardening celebrity, Georgina Woodhouse (played commandingly by Helen Mirren). On Georgina Woodhouse's recommendation, the prisoners are invited to create a garden for the annual Hampton Court Flower Show. The result is my favorite part of the movie: a profusion of wildflowers growing out of a rusted, wrecked car beneath an underpass. It comes complete with a road sign warning: "Caution: Wildflowers Ahead," which I liked so well I've used it as a chapter subheading in this book.

Sure, these are not the varieties of wildflowers that prosper in our Arizona yard, but the movie does convey the beauty of a garden that is informal and rough around the edges. It also gives you some idea of how seriously, and I mean like a blood sport, the British take gardening. After watching *Greenfingers,* it occurs to me that most Americans could stand to put a lot more gusto into gardening. It also occurs to me that watching the deep green English countryside flicker by on the silver screen in the middle of the dry and spiny Sonoran Desert is about the strangest possible way to spend an evening.

There is a novelty about watching a movie outdoors, a fact that drive-in theaters used to capitalize on. With the closure of many drive-ins, the outdoor movie as an American tradition is fast disappearing, but garden cinema keeps the tradition alive. It also lets you supervise a teenage daughter in a way you could never do if she were in a car with a boy at the drive-in. With my daughter rapidly approaching her teens, this thought comforts me. I just have to make sure the futon stays upright.

Sleeping Outdoors

It was really an old Arizona idea. In the 1920s and 30s, before air conditioning, Arizonans regularly slept outdoors in summer. Many older homes had screened sleeping porches, sometimes called Arizona rooms. For us, our northeast courtyard became kitchen, dining room, theater, and bedroom.

The piece of furniture that made the bedroom possible was a simple wooden futon with a slipcover. The futon, usually a college kid's couch and bed, is not meant for outdoor use. However, our little alcove is tucked away from the elements just enough to allow us to bring a little indoor furniture outside. To further protect the wood from the elements, we applied a good primer and two coats of lavender paint to match the house trim. We selected a heavy denim slipcover that we could wash after dust storms. Our futon turned out to be an ideal piece of garden furniture. During lazy afternoons, Deirdre and Zoë would read magazines outside. On weekends, I would often come home from work for lunch and find Deirdre and Zoë napping on the futon.

For Deirdre and me, sleeping outdoors put a spark in our fourteen-year-old marriage. There was something seductive about sneaking outdoors after we had Zoë asleep. Because the futon is tucked into a little alcove, it feels private, like a three-sided cabin on the deck of a ship adjacent to a garden with a roof of stars. In the daytime, the alcove is semiprivate; at night, it feels as secluded as a wilderness area.

Above the futon hangs one of the great enigmas and curiosities of our front yard: the birdcage skeleton good-luck charm. Another treasure I unearthed in a salvage yard, our birdcage skeleton good-luck charm didn't have an auspicious beginning. First of all, we found it at Gerson's salvage yard, which for our budget has become a bit gentrified and high-priced. Secondly, our birdcage was not really a birdcage at all. It was a big

Zoë finds the alcove a good place for homework.

boa-constrictor cage complete with a beat-up reptile heater painted baby-poop brown. It took some explaining before Deirdre caught my vision for the birdcage.

"We'll retrofit it. I'll paint it red," I said enthusiastically. "And maybe we could put chickens in it," I added, knowing this was my ace in the hole. Deirdre loves chickens, and just the thought of a hen clucking around in the cage helped win her over.

We never did put chickens in the cage. We did paint it red. We also bought a pair of Australian diamond doves that escaped from the cage several times before permanently disappearing into the mesquite bosque near our house. After spending around $80 on doves, we began to consider less-animate objects for the cage. A sombrero-wearing papier-mâché Day of the Dead skeleton seemed to fit the bill. He smiles 365 days a year, is a light eater, and hasn't flown the coop yet.

Within the crescent-shaped bed between the north patio and the wall we put these plants, some of which, especially the cacti, are in pots:

Trees
- tenaza

Shrubs
- Baja fairy duster, Chihuahuan orchid shrub, Superstition mallow

Perennials and annual wildflowers
- autumn sage, bat-faced cuphea, firecracker penstemon, Goodding's verbena, lemon sundrops, Mt. Lemmon marigold, Sonoran nightshade, spreading fleabane, Texas violet sage, tufted evening primrose

Agaves, cacti, and yuccas
- artichoke agave, bishop's cap, 'Blue Elf' aloe, blue yucca, claret cup cactus, Indian fig prickly pear,

'Los Angeles' torch cactus, Mexican fencepost cactus, Mexican hairy barrel, owl's eyes, ponytail palm, Queen Victoria agave, slipper plant, soft-tipped agave, Weber's agave

Plants we used in the wild area outside the wall on our north patio:

Trees
- Chilean mesquite, foothills palo verde, ocotillo

Shrubs
- brittlebush, fragrant ranger, jojoba, pink fairy duster, 'Silver Peso' Texas mountain laurel

Cacti, agaves, and accents
- Arizona queen of the night, Baja "punk rock hairdo" barrel cactus, desert spoon, dinner plate prickly pear, Engelmann's prickly pear, fishhook barrel, Gentry's agave, mescal ceniza, ocahui agave, Parry's agave, Santa Rita prickly pear, tuxedo spine prickly pear, twin flowered agave, variegated century plant

Perennial and annual wildflowers
- Arizona poppy, bat-faced cuphea, canyon penstemon, Colorado four o'clock, damianita daisy, desert bluebells, desert marigold, desert senna, dogweed, firecracker penstemon, firewheel, giant snapdragon, globemallow, Goodding's verbena, lemon sundrops, Mexican gold poppy, Mexican hat, Mt. Lemmon marigold, Parry's penstemon, prickly poppy, rock penstemon, Sonoran justicia, Sonoran nightshade, succulent lupine, superb penstemon, Texas betony

Vines
- twining snapdragon, yellow orchid vine

attracting and repelling wildlife

attracting and repelling wildlife—gardening in the wild-urban interface

One night in early June, we were sleeping out on the futon. An early monsoon storm had just blown through, leaving the air fresh and cool and filled with the smell of creosote bush, and it seemed an ideal night for sleeping outdoors.

We had worked hard all day and fell asleep quickly. Then around eleven, loud chomping and snorting noises just outside the garden gate awakened us.

There had been telltale signs of javelinas in the garden before, but I had never caught them in the act. Javelinas, or peccaries, are medium-sized boar-like animals with wiry salt-and-pepper hair and piglike snouts—technically they are not pigs, but many locals call them that. Native to Arizona, they have notoriously poor vision and usually travel in groups. When we were building the house, I left a partially eaten box of chocolate-covered Dunkin' Donuts sitting on our then-unfinished kitchen counter

one night. The next morning I found chocolate smeared across the floor, punctuated with small hoof marks.

I walked quietly to the garden wall and peered over it into the darkness. I could make out the forms of two large, black, hairy pigs eating something near my foothills palo verde tree. They were unbelievably loud. What kind of wild animal can make this much noise and not get eaten by predators? Where were the mountain lions when I needed them? Deirdre remarked that they were noisier than Zoë eating Cap'n Crunch cereal. I wanted to

Cleaning penstemon seeds on the kitchen table (opposite); cherry sage (inset); desert bluebells (pages 138–139).

photograph them, so I went inside to get my camera. I took a couple of digital flash pictures in which only the eyes of the hoofed devils were visible among the desert marigolds. On closer inspection, it appeared that these marauders were ripping the pads off my Indian fig prickly pear cacti. These plants, which I had grown from infancy, had just reached almost five feet tall, and I was counting on them soon to fulfill their intended purpose: screening. But our garden had turned into a javelina cantina.

This got my dander up, and I told Deirdre I was going to herd them off the property, an idea she considered unwise. Dressed in only a beat-up pair of khaki shorts and Teva river sandals, I cagily made my way down the desert pathway armed with a police-issue flashlight and a good-sized rock. I knew that javelinas were half-blind and had sharp teeth that they would use on you if they got riled up, especially if they had piglets with them. My brain was trying to reconstruct the size of the two shapes I had seen in the dark. Was one of them really considerably larger than the other? Were they acting like family members? Before I was a few hundred feet down the path, I had convinced myself that the big pig was the mother and the smaller the baby. I was half expecting Big Momma to come charging out from behind a brittlebush and latch her big canines onto my calf like a pit bull. As I shuffled down the wet desert path, I felt a cool breeze in my shorts and realized that my fly was unzipped; this triggered an even more unpleasant thought about a possible location for a peccary bite. I'd heard plenty of suburban myths about javelina bites. Rumor had it that, like a gator bite, a javelina bite was a dirty injury that often led to infection and sometimes to the loss of a limb. But as any committed gardener will understand, losing a limb seemed a small price to pay for

Texas betony blooms fiery red beneath a foothills palo verde.

saving some good specimen evergreen screening plants. I was intent on driving the pigs out of our garden.

I thought I had them in a bottleneck between my garden wall and my neighbors', but the crafty swine were quiet when they weren't eating. With wide sweeps of my flashlight, I was unable to locate a single sow or piglet. All I heard was the faint click of a hoof on a rock in the distance. I had been foiled by Peccary.

Besides pig murder, I considered my options. I could fence them out with a somewhat camouflaged net fence. I had seen this used at the Arizona-Sonora Desert Museum. It was a lot less obtrusive than the orange limit fencing they use in alpine skiing events, but you couldn't call it invisible. Another solution was to put a circular chicken-wire fence around each individual plant. This was also unattractive, but functional. I had seen this done at a new city library, and the resulting plants grew in a column shape to match their containers.

All things considered, I didn't want to fence my yard. After all, the peccaries were only eating Indian figs. Since the Indian figs were already ruined, I chose to pull them out and replace them with more pig-resistant plants.

I considered using a psychotropic columnar cactus called the San Pedro. This multi-armed organ-pipe-shaped cactus was a favorite hallucinogen of South American indigenous peoples and curious, wayward American teenagers. I hoped that if the pigs ate it, it would induce bad swine trips that would prevent further ingestion. Of course, there was the possibility that they could become addicted and organize themselves into a crazed gang. They might even have turf wars over the San Pedro. The thought made me shudder.

My next thought was to plant another large prickly pear-type plant, the dinner plate or clockface, which had more thorns than the Indian fig. These thorns, which might cause discomfort in a javelina jowl, were a plus. The enormous round pads of the dinner plate prickly pear are true to their name, and the asymmetrical form of the plant would be attractive in our garden. Finding them was another issue. I finally tracked some down at a lonely cactus nursery on the edge of town. They had been there so long that the plants had rooted through the holes in their pots into the ground. It was the morning after a heavy rain, and the pads were thick and swollen with water. The specimens I bought were unbelievably heavy, and I had to wrestle them into the car and pack newspaper around the outer pads to keep the clock-face-sized pads from breaking off at their joints.

The dinner plates proved javelina-proof for a full year, until one July night two big pads were unceremoniously felled by hoofed marauders. Deirdre noticed the next morning but didn't mention it to me for several days, knowing that I was now consumed with managing a cuter and fluffier foe.

The first year we lived in our home we scarcely saw a rabbit and enjoyed desert bluebell displays galore. By the second year, the occasional cottontail would appear, and by the third year the sight of rabbits was common. I was readying the garden for a spring tour, and the rabbits began to concern me. In a friend's garden, I had seen their handiwork on his bluebell and penstemon stalks, and I was determined to prevent this, even if that meant doing it Elmer Fudd style. Zoë had read *Watership Down* several times and was convinced that rabbits had names like Hazel and Blackberry and could talk to each other. She was ecstatic that rabbits had taken up residence in the front garden. This meant that any truly barbaric eradication efforts on my part would have to be covert. I began with a simple and perhaps stupid strategy of making a decoy area. Using excess reclaimed water, I made a lush area filled with native flowers just across the path from my precious penstemons and bluebells. My hope was the rabbits would never leave this leafy shelter until they were rooted out and eaten by packs of coyotes.

The tactic did succeed in keeping bunnies from *living* in my yard, but it did not prevent them from visiting. In fact, I had created a great oasis of rabbit living much too close to my front garden. Luckily, most of my native plants were just not that attractive to the rabbits—not even the plants in my "decoy" area. They much preferred the potted pansies in my neighbor's yard, which resembled a fine French mesclun salad. In contrast, my agaves and pungent damianita daisy must have tasted like rope and cat pee.

When it comes to a rabbit-coyote confrontation, I always cheer for the coyote—a sort of wild hero of mine. I think of him, the notorious trickster, as a dog too smart to have a master. When I run around the perimeter of our development in the early morning, I see coyotes standing at the edges of civilization. Sometimes they just stare at me; other times they are pestered by ravens. One evening, as I was riding my bicycle home from work, I saw a coyote standing still as a statue near a roll-off dumpster on a vacant lot. I had a sudden urge to catch the trickster, perhaps even domesticate him. He was only twenty feet from me. I pointed my mountain bike wheel at a spot between his eyes and stood on the pedals. The coyote, like a dog, went down on his front paws and then jumped away from me. He dodged right, and then left. I was hot on his trail, but he managed to elude me by running circles around the dumpster. After a few minutes, our little game ceased to amuse him, and he trotted off to a distant hill. At the top of the little rise, he paused, turning his head as if to give this crazy bastard one last parting glance.

A big dumb guy on a bike was no challenge for him. In my heart of hearts, I knew that the coyote only wanted rabbits or small, sausage-shaped dogs with

Damianita daisy.

high-pitched barks. He desired a good, clean cottontail rabbit chase on open desert. Once he caught the rabbit, the coyote would tear open the soft white belly and slurp up the rabbit's pink steaming guts—guts that might even contain some of my fresh penstemon stalks. To see coyotes in my yard offered a great sign of hope. It meant that in some respect, nature was in balance. The rabbits couldn't get too comfortable in their little burrows if coyotes were near. Some of my wildflowers might actually bloom before their stalks were unceremoniously felled beneath some twitching nose.

At night when the yip-yip-yip of coyotes sounds near my house, I smile to myself. "Tonight," I think, "the coyotes have won. One less hungry rabbit to browse my plants!"

Other predatory carnivores give me hope that the rabbit population will stay in check. At the nursery, just a block from my house, I once scared up a full-grown bobcat sleeping in a shady corner among some five-gallon natal plum plants. He was almost as surprised to see me as I was to see him. With great agility, he bounded around the nursery's perimeter fence, looking for an opening. Evidently he had forgotten how he got in. We later found him lounging under a table of cacti. The next morning he was gone. I've never seen the silent and secretive bobcat in our yard, but I imagine that he visits at night, crouching beneath a brittlebush, poised for cottontail meat.

As much as I would like to see rabbit-eating bobcats prowling my yard, I recognize that human-wildcat interaction, or more accurately, predation of humans by mountain lions, has become a major issue for wildlife managers. In early 2004, the most popular recreation area in southern Arizona, Sabino Canyon, was temporarily closed on account of these big cats. According to the Arizona Game and Fish Department,

Engelmann's prickly pear engulfed by Goodding's verbena.

the lions began stalking people who used the paved trail for running and hiking. The cougars seemed to have lost their fear of humans. State officials, already on guard by a suit brought against the state for a bear mauling on Mt. Lemmon, were quick to close the canyon. This situation seemed to be moving toward a bad result—especially if you were a mountain lion or an avid hiker. As events unfolded, Game and Fish tried to hunt, and later to relocate, the problem lions, while Earth First! protesters hid in the canyon and planted lion scent to throw off the hunters' dogs. The problem didn't present any easy answers; one lion was shot and others were moved to a Scottsdale facility.

By definition, the wilderness is an unpredictable place. Our lives have become insulated from the natural world, and our urban landscapes are partly to blame. Luckily, bringing fauna a few notches down the food chain from the cougar into your yard is a lot easier than managing a recreation area full of people and emaciated big cats. While you wouldn't want a mountain lion den under your patio table, leaving space in the yard for the horned toad, hummingbird, and occasional rock squirrel ought to be the price of admission for living in the big garden called the Sonoran Desert.

At night we see birds of prey. A great horned owl perches on a nearby roof, and his quiet white wings often cast moon shadows on our patio. For a gardener with rabbit problems, the sight of an owl is the most reassuring thing in the world; the only death an owl foreshadows is that of the hungry rabbit or rock squirrel.

When we swim at the community pool at night, great numbers of nighthawks, sometimes more than twenty at a time, swoop overhead, battling with the bats for insects. It turns out that the pool makes the perfect hunting ground for the nighthawk. Unlike a bat guided by sonar, the nighthawk is crepuscular —that is, it needs some light to see. The pool lights have the added benefit of attracting myriad insects. If you float on your back and look up from the glow of the pool, the flight of the nighthawks is as beautiful as any ballet and as daring as air-show aerobatics.

Most gardeners are bent on attracting hummingbirds to their gardens; we were no exception. Little did we know that these iridescent featherweights would turn into back-yard thugs. One bright May morning Deirdre called me into her office: "Scott, come here—you've got to see this." Through the twin double-hung windows behind Deirdre's desk, I saw a hummingbird

Gregg's mist flower.

fitfully tailing a queen butterfly (*Danaus gillipus*) as she made her rounds on the stamens of fluffy blue Gregg's mist flower. It was not that the hummingbird was interested in the Gregg's mist flower; it was more that the hummingbird was intent on getting that interloping butterfly out of his space. The butterfly, of course, was as oblivious to the hummingbird's interruption as a blonde trophy wife at a Nordstrom's shoe sale. The hummingbird was getting more and more annoyed, performing a series of high-speed approaches that finally drove the butterfly around the corner. At this point, the hummingbird went back and sat in his favorite chuparosa bush, like a pit bull guarding a rib-eye steak, keeping his eye out for the butterfly. After only a short time, the butterfly reappeared and the hummingbird flew back into action, following the butterfly just a couple of inches behind. The tenacity of this hummingbird led me to believe it would not think twice about skewering that butterfly's wings with his beak.

A couple of mornings later, I found a dead queen butterfly suspended in the lacy foliage of the Gregg's mist flower. Its luminescent wings resembled a thin shard of stained glass. They glowed orange and black in the morning light. I couldn't help but wonder if the hummingbird had somehow done it in.

Out in the front garden, a family of rock squirrels took up residence in a PVC drainage pipe near our palo verde. Barely bigger than chipmunks, the squirrels seemed more interested in seeds than in plants, and they loved to hoard the plentiful foothills palo verde seeds. My attitude toward the squirrels was much better than my attitude toward the rabbits.

Some of the most hair-raising encounters in my garden have been with reptiles, rattlesnakes in particular. When a neighbor informed me that she had just seen a rattlesnake crawl into my driveway one hot

Our Mexican tin-can disco ball.

summer night, I went outside with my flashlight to investigate. In my normal stupid outfit of shorts and no shoes, I walked around on my driveway shining the flashlight into nooks and crannies. I was standing with my big toes hanging over the edge of the concrete apron when I happened to shine my light down and noticed a fine young *Crotalus atrox* (Western diamondback) lying against the concrete. Very quickly, I jumped back away from the edge, went inside, and called various Rural Metro firehouses and animal rescue lines, none of which would remove my snake. My neighbor from across the street, who has three young daughters, came over and suggested that we kill it. When I was growing up in a former Arizona ranching family, this was how we always dealt with rattlesnakes. My dad and uncle killed rattlesnakes without a second thought. I'm sorry to say that I decapitated that rattler with two quick blows from the blade of a garden hoe. It was bad behavior for someone who advocates wild gardens.

Gardeners have one really good reason not to kill rattlesnakes: they eat mammals that eat plants. Next time, I will move the snake. I've already prepared some long tongs and a trash can with a lid ready in the garage. The only really interesting thing that came out of killing the snake was watching how fast and thoroughly the ants devoured the snake's flesh. Within forty-eight hours, the snake was nothing but an S-curve of white bones.

Speaking of ants, the most efficient ant vacuum I know is the regal horned lizard, which is just a fancy name for the horny toad. Although a large swarming ant mound can bite a horned lizard to death, he usually just sits there like a stone unless the ants get really agitated, in which case he runs away. One summer morning, I found a corpulent horned lizard in my front yard. I picked him up in my hand and set him near a large army-ant mound that had become something of an annoyance because of its close proximity to

a path. I had often caught horny toads as a boy, so I recognized this one as a very large specimen. He filled my entire palm and from head to tail was as long as my hand with my fingers extended. When I set him down, he didn't waste any time and began to lap up ants by the dozen. The ants would crawl over his head until they reached the precipice of his mouth, at which point a quick flick of the tongue rendered the ant into breakfast. This fine and truly regal animal was an ant-eating vacuum camouflaged as a rock.

Our favorite amphibious visitor wasn't a horned toad but a *real* toad. The Sonoran Desert toad (*Bufo alvarius,* also known as the Colorado River toad) is a stern and portly beast that makes a grand appearance only after our summer rains begin. One hot August night, I looked out at Deirdre's fountain and noticed something was awry. A massive glistening toad was perched on the ledge of Deirdre's water feature, staring at his reflection in the mirrored door behind the fountain. The toad squatted about a foot away from the blue and yellow ceramic frog that served as the spigot for our fountain. Silently, I crept outside in stocking feet to try to take a picture and observe this oddity. I couldn't decide if he was confused by the mirror and was trying to woo himself or if he was trying to court the ceramic frog from Guanajuato. Either way, it was a frustrating situation for a big old desert toad looking to hook up with a female of the same species. After I approached him a little too close with the camera, he hopped off the fountain lip and disappeared behind a stack of bricks.

I've always considered a monsoon storm a sexy event, but the point was driven home one night after a subtropical rumbler dropped an inch of rain in a little over half an hour. Deirdre, Zoë, and I walked around the neighborhood following the *mwaa-mwaa* sound of

Spreading fleabane, sundrops, moss verbena, and tufted evening primrose.

ARIZONA
BWZ 146
GRAND CANYON STATE
MM 6747
UTAH
TS-3953
19 COLORADO 72
UTAH
025 ZKU
ARIZONA 52
P 6
ARIZONA 64
FGH-208
GRAND CANYON STATE
Ski Utah!
247 KDN
GREATEST SNOW ON EARTH
AHS
Colorado
CIVANO
LARIMER

toads trying to find mates. Their song, which sounds like bleating sheep, led us to a retention basin full of rainwater and Couch's spadefoot toads (*Scaphiopus couchi*) having a toad orgy. Spadefoots burrow underground, listening for a certain low-frequency vibration (caused by rain and thunder) that signals the time to come out, find a pond, and breed. We watched them floating around, stacked on top of each other all over the surface of the pond. The whole pond was oozing with life in an urgent song and dance performed by the warty hordes. The scene gave new meaning to the phrase "Mr. Toad's wild ride." These were not the well-reasoned toads of Beatrix Potter's children's books: these were toads gone wild.

Even though the Colorado River toad secretes poisonous mucus containing a toxin called bufotenine, which induces powerful hallucinations and possible death when ingested, I consider them a gardener's best pet. They eat prodigious amounts of beetles that would otherwise be boring into your desert trees. The spadefoot toad also enjoys eating beetles but prefers them garnished with termites that would otherwise be eating your house. Since everyone except dogs and small children is quite capable of avoiding toad-licking, I think that every desert gardener should create a moist, shady place for a toad or two to make a home. Given the fact that the Colorado River toad lives at least ten years, a toad could be a long-term garden resident.

Encounters with rattlesnakes and toads aren't that uncommon in the desert—but they were uncommon to me. They made me reflect about the exquisite characteristics of the animals that evolved in this sun-filled place—animals that make a perfect match for the rugged and varied landscape of the desert West. I am amazed at how many creatures have found a niche in

our tiny yard. Last Tuesday morning, I watched a young Cooper's hawk (*Accipter cooperii*) perched in our palo verde, hunting the rock squirrel that lives in the pipe beneath it. Moments later, after the hawk had given up, a mother Gambel's quail (*Callipepla gambelii*) and her brood emerged from a dense patch of Goodding's verbena near our front door and strutted across the path as if to say, "You won't be messing with *these* babies, Mr. Hawk." I saw whiptail lizards basking in the sun on our adobe wall and heard the tenaza tree off the patio buzzing with carpenter bees.

If you look at desert cities like Tucson from the air, you might conclude that development has irrevocably ruined much of the desert. The streets and buildings are lined up in neat grids like chips on a circuit board. The familiar saguaro-dotted hillsides are fewer, and the houses are everywhere. It appears that in the fight to save this unique desert environment, we have lost a lot of ground, but what we forget is that in all those new subdivisions, the ground is still there. Thousands of little eighth-acre lots are created. Some new homeowner will be gaining ground. Each of these lots is ripe with possibilities. There is a chance to remake a semblance of the desert. Of course, these little lots can't support big game like deer, cougars, and bears, but a lot of little desert plants and animals can fit on your average lot. On our little eighth of an acre, we've proven to ourselves that desert isn't the exclusive province of national parks and federal lands. The desert is a mindset. It is not bound by fences or roadways or canals; it is discriminated against out of people's prejudices and re-created, often in glorious detail, by people's love for it. Desert plants and animals are looking for a niche, a niche we were able to create in our sun-filled yard.

Twining snapdragon winds through our ocotillo fence and license plate collection.

afterword

Two months prior to a photo shoot of our garden by *Sunset* magazine, I was out in the front yard pruning my foothills palo verde tree. Using a folding serrated pruning saw, I was cutting out branches infested with mistletoe. I had been up and down a ladder all morning, and most of the hard work was done. I took a few steps back to admire my work and saw one partially hollow branch that needed removal. Using the razor-sharp pruning saw, I attacked the rather thick branch, which gave way more easily than I expected; I looked down in disbelief to find that I had nearly sawed off my left index finger. For a moment, I cursed my stupidity and watched drops of my blood falling on the orange clay.

Deirdre drove me to the emergency room, where they determined that I had cut a tendon. They stitched me up and prescribed eight weeks of physical therapy along with a bottle of the highly addictive painkiller Percocet, a Rush Limbaugh favorite. I was told by a coworker that the medication had a street value of $30 a pill, which seemed to me reason enough to avoid taking it unless the pain became unbearable.

As it turned out, the Percocet was superfluous; the only drug I needed was gardening. By the afternoon of my accident, I was out pruning again with my finger bandaged up like a fat white sausage. I had to get back on the horse. I did not resent the saw or my tree—I took full responsibility for nearly severing my finger. Sometimes our scars define us. It sounds a little hokey, but I like to think that at the moment the saw cut my flesh, I became one with my palo verde tree. It was a nasty cut, and the saw was full of bright green bits of palo verde bark. I imagined flecks of chartreuse palo verde cambium coursing through my veins like powerful green glitter. I fancied that this might be the event that would make me a gardening superhero, a cross between Green Lantern, the Incredible Hulk, and Sir Terence Conran. Although I didn't turn green and all-powerful, to my family's amazement I gardened well into the afternoon with my bandaged, claw-like left hand.

That evening, I pulled up one of the Sunset chairs I had made and sat on the porch in the golden afternoon light. I admired galvanized buckets full of plants we had cut back sitting next to me on the porch. Zoë pulled up a seat next to me. Deirdre was deadheading the last of the desert marigolds under the canopy of our freshly shaped palo verde. In spite of my injury, I was happy. My garden was full, as was my life. The people and things I loved best were close at hand. Our awful, rocky, clay soil was dotted with the rosettes of young penstemons. Since we had begun, the yard was different and the same. It was a little less wild than it had been, but not completely domesticated. It recalled a lush piece of desert before the rains faltered. More than anything, it was a garden set against the canvas of a big Arizona sky. It was, and is, a yard full of sun.

"Snow-capped" pincushion cactus.

acknowledgments

I would like to thank my parents, Wayne and Catherine Calhoun, who taught me to follow my dreams; Ross Humphreys, for photographing much of the project and believing in it from the beginning; Susan Lowell, for her unfailing wit and insight into this manuscript; Lisa Cooper, whose relentless editing and sharp banter flushed out many vagaries and redundancies; the Shipley family, for offering me a career in the nursery business; Janet Rademacher, for proudly displaying junk in her garden; Carrie Nimmer, for sharing her passion for garden design; and Charles Mann, for his pioneering work schlepping through desert gardens looking for a good photo.

The following quotations were used with permission: Henry Mitchell quote on p. 5 © 1998 Henry Mitchell, from *Henry Mitchell on Gardening,* reprinted by permission of Houghton Mifflin Co.; Larry McMurtry quotes on pp. 9 and 35 courtesy Larry McMurtry; Lauren Springer quote on p. 30 © 1994 Lauren Springer, from *The Undaunted Garden,* reprinted by permission of Fulcrum Press; Jim Knopf quote on p. 31 © 1991 Jim Knopf, from *The Xeriscape Flower Gardener,* reprinted by permission of Johnson Books; Derek Jarman quote on p. 37 © 1996 Derek Jarman, from *Derek Jarman's Garden,* reprinted by permission of Donadio & Olson Inc.; Terry Tempest Williams quote on p. 39 © 2001 Terry Tempest Williams, from *Red: Passion and Patience in the Desert,* reprinted by permission of Pantheon; Mary Irish quote on p. 46 © 2000 Mary Irish, from *Gardening in the Desert,* reprinted by permission of University of Arizona Press; Charles Bowden quote on p. 49 courtesy Charles Bowden; Judy Mielke quote on p. 50 courtesy Judy Mielke; Edward Abbey quotes on pp. 53, 56, and 110 courtesy Clarke Abbey; Verlyn Klinkenborg quote on p. 68 courtesy Verlyn Klinkenborg; Rick Darke quote on p. 73 © 2002 Rick Darke, from *The American Woodland Garden,* reprinted by permission of Timber Press; Michael Pollan quote on p. 74 courtesy Michael Pollan; Bruce Berger quote on p. 83 courtesy Bruce Berger; Woody Guthrie lyrics p. 132 from "California Stars," © 1998 Woody Guthrie Publications Inc. and reprinted with permission. All rights reserved. The chapter "Building the Sonoran Bungalow" was adapted from an article that appeared in the spring/summer 2002 issue of *Terrain.org: A Journal of the Built & Natural Environment.*

After the fragrant tenaza blooms, its cream flowers dry to butter yellow (opposite); Superstition mallow (pages 158–159).

appendixes

appendix A:
thirteen steps to creating outdoor spaces you will want to live in

1. Make an "A, B, and C" priority list of plants, accessories, and activities that you want in your garden. The A list is for must-have garden items, the B list for things you would like if at all possible, the C list for things you want but probably can't afford.

2. Draw a "mind-map" of your garden. Using your A, B, and C lists, begin drawing three sizes of circles: large circles for A items, medium circles for B items, and small circles for C items. Connect the circles with lines to show how they connect. Think more about the A, B, and C items. Start crossing out items that seem less important, and embellish the more important ones. For example, if a hummingbird garden becomes important, start making a list of hummingbird plants or feeders that you like. Draw sketches and pictures if it helps. At this point, don't worry about where things will go on your lot. When you finish your mind map, you should have a handful of items that you are very excited about.

3. On a large sheet of paper, draw a plan in pencil that shows your lot and house and any walkways, trees, and walls. Now, laying a sheet of vellum, tissue, or other semi-transparent paper on top of your drawing, begin drawing circles that show where your big ideas could go. Be flexible and try different activities in different places to see how they work. When you have settled on where each item goes, move to step four.

4. Draw your hardscapes first. Working generally from large features to small, place the major hardscape elements of your design. Think of your design as a series of small gardens within a larger landscape. The smaller gardens are like chapters of a good novel, with the entire landscape as the novel. Like the chapters in a novel, each area tells a story that relates to the whole.

5. Use the position of the sun seasonally and during the course of the day to drive your design. For example, if you like to eat dinner outdoors in the summer, aim for

an eastern or northeastern exposure for a dining table. For outdoor dining in the winter, a southern exposure will keep you and your guests comfortable.

6. Don't underestimate the need for shade and seating. No one is going to stand in the June sun and have a conversation or eat a muffin. You need to provide shady nooks. These could be under trees, umbrellas, or vine-covered pergolas. Seating can be built in or portable. Portable seating may allow you to use an area for more than one activity.

7. If you are planning sports courts, pools, etc., do some research on their size and proper orientation. For example, volleyball, tennis, and basketball courts should be oriented with their long axes running north and south. You need to know the minimum size of each feature for comfort and use.

8. Connect all the areas by a circulation pattern. For example, how will you get to your outdoor dining area from the kitchen?

9. Consider if and how you will enclose spaces. The heights of walls, trellises, and ramadas need to suit both functionality and aesthetics. For instance, if you want a small oasis garden area with perennials, you may need to wall the garden to keep rabbits out. In our case, we wanted to sleep outside without waking up in the middle of the night with javelina snouts in our faces. This required an enclosed area.

10. Pay special attention to the walkways and transition areas such as gates and steps, making sure they are wide enough. If you're an avid gardener, make sure openings are wide enough for a wheelbarrow. Paths narrower than three feet will not allow people to walk two abreast. Make your pathways as generous as possible.

11. Choose a theme and layout in harmony with the architecture of your home and express it by using a few carefully chosen materials. Make sure your garden doesn't look like the building materials display at Home Depot. Your theme should carry all the way through your design, from your hardscape choices to your pot styles. For example, if your house has brick trim, you may want to use the same color and style of brick in a patio. If your house uses a trim color you like, consider painting your pots to match or choose pots in complementary colors.

12. Plants are the last things you place in your design, but they can make or break it. You need to have a theme for the plant palette so it doesn't end up looking like the dog's dinner. A pine tree and a saguaro are not going to jibe; stick with a theme that includes desert-adapted plants. For example, you could do a Chihuahuan Desert theme, a Baja theme, a Great Basin theme, or a Mojave Desert theme.

13. Decorate your garden as you would your home. Use antiques, photos, handmade objects—anything that conforms to the themes and colors of the garden. Shop for unique items. Keep in mind that the garden is never finished. Like us, it is always evolving, maturing, and changing.

appendix B:
a chart of indispensable desert plants

A Note about Latin and Common Plant Names

Gardening is one of the few hobbies in America that requires its participants to know a little Latin. And if we have to learn a bushel of Latin plant names, it would be nice if they didn't change every few years.

During the time this book was written, taxonomists changed many of the botanical names of desert plants. Some of the most notable changes occurred in the palo verde family, which went from the *Cercidium* genus to the *Parkinsonia* genus, except for the Mexican palo verde, which did the reverse. Sound confusing? It is. Although botanical names are meant to provide a scientific reference to a particular plant, when botanical names change often, they may seem less reliable than common names. However, since common names are even more variable (one common name may refer to several different plants, and the same plant may have several names that vary from region to region),

botanical names are the only game in town for accurate identification.

With this in mind, we have made every attempt to list the plants in this book by their most frequently used common name(s) and by their currently accepted botanical name, with old but still-used botanical names in parentheses beside the accepted name in the following chart. Because nurseries are often understandably wary of changing botanical names on their signage and retraining their employees, the new names often take decades to make their way into your local garden center, so you may need to search for these plants by their old botanical names. In the meantime, I'll be doing my damnedest to remember that the new name for Texas ebony is *Ebenopsis ebano*.

TREES

COMMON NAME	BOTANICAL NAME	COLD HARDINESS (°F)	FLOWER COLOR
ARIZONA ASH	*Fraxinus velutina*	−10	insignificant flowers
ARIZONA SYCAMORE	*Platanus wrightii*	−10	insignificant flowers
BERLANDIER ACACIA, GUAJILLO	*Acacia berlandieri*	15	cream yellow
BLUE PALO VERDE	*Parkinsonia florida (Cercidium floridum)*	15	bright yellow
BOOJUM TREE	*Fouquieria columnaris*	25	pale yellow
'BUBBA' DESERT WILLOW	*Chilopsis linearis* 'Bubba'	0	pink
CATCLAW ACACIA	*Acacia greggii*	0	light yellow-green
CHILEAN MESQUITE	*Prosopis chilensis*	15	cream
'DARK STORM' DESERT WILLOW	*Chilopsis linearis* 'Dark Storm'	0	deep burgundy
FOOTHILLS PALO VERDE	*Parkinsonia microphyllum (Cercidium microphyllum)*	15	sulfur yellow
'HOPE' DESERT WILLOW	*Chilopsis linearis* 'Hope'	0	white
IRONWOOD	*Olneya tesota*	20	mauve
'LOIS ADAMS' DESERT WILLOW	*Chilopsis linearis* 'Lois Adams'	0	dark and light pink, podless
'LUCRETIA HAMILTON' DESERT WILLOW	*Chilopsis linearis* 'Lucretia Hamilton'	0	burgundy
OCOTILLO, COACH WHIP	*Fouquieria splendens*	10	red
PALO BLANCO	*Acacia willardiana*	variable, 19–28	cream yellow
PALO BREA	*Parkinsonia praecox (Cercidium praecox)*	25	bright yellow
'REGAL' DESERT WILLOW	*Chilopsis linearis* 'Regal'	0	bicolored pink and burgundy

Trees (continued)

COMMON NAME	BOTANICAL NAME	COLD HARDINESS (°F)	FLOWER COLOR
SWEET ACACIA	*Acacia farnesiana (A. smallii)*	10	bright yellow
TENAZA	*Harvardia pallens (Pithecellobium pallens)*	10	creamy white
'TIMELESS BEAUTY' DESERT WILLOW	*Chilopsis linearis* 'Timeless Beauty'	0	bicolored pink and burgundy, podless
VELVET MESQUITE, ARIZONA NATIVE MESQUITE	*Prosopis juliflora (P. velutina)*	0	cream yellow
'WARREN JONES' DESERT WILLOW	*Chilopsis linearis* 'Warren Jones'	0	large, pink
'WHITE STORM' DESERT WILLOW	*Chilopsis linearis* 'White Storm'	0	white
'WONDERFUL' POMEGRANATE	*Punica granatum* 'Wonderful'	15	red-orange

SHRUBS

COMMON NAME	BOTANICAL NAME	COLD HARDINESS (°F)	FLOWER COLOR
BAJA FAIRY DUSTER	*Calliandra californica*	20	red
BRITTLEBUSH	*Encelia farinosa*	15	bright yellow
CHIHUAHUAN ORCHID SHRUB, ORCHID TREE	*Bauhinia lunaroides (B. congesta)*	15	white
CHUPAROSA	*Justicia californica*	20	red
CREOSOTE BUSH	*Larrea tridentata*	5	yellow
FRAGRANT RANGER	*Leucophyllum pruinosum*	10	grape purple
JOJOBA	*Simmondsia chinensis*	15	insignificant flowers
PINK FAIRY DUSTER	*Calliandra eriophylla*	0	pink

Shrubs (continued)

COMMON NAME	BOTANICAL NAME	COLD HARDINESS (°F)	FLOWER COLOR
'SIERRA BOUQUET' RANGER	*Leucophyllum pruinosum* 'Sierra Bouquet'	10	grape purple
'SILVER CLOUD' TEXAS RANGER	*Leucophyllum candidum* 'Silver Cloud'	10	purple
'SILVER PESO' TEXAS MOUNTAIN LAUREL	*Sophora secundiflora* 'Silver Peso'	15	true blue
SILVER SAGE	*Artemisia ludviciana*	−30	insignificant
SOUTHWEST CORAL BEAN	*Erythrina flabelliformis*	28	red
SUPERSTITION MALLOW, INDIAN MALLOW	*Abutilon palmeri*	25	yellow-orange
TURPENTINE BUSH	*Ericameria laricifolia*	0	yellow
YELLOW CHUPAROSA	*Justicia californica* 'Yellow'	20	butter yellow

PERENNIALS, WILDFLOWERS, AND GRASSES

COMMON NAME	BOTANICAL NAME	COLD HARDINESS (°F)	FLOWER COLOR
ARIZONA LUPINE	*Lupinus arizonicus*	annual	blue
ARIZONA POPPY	*Kallstroemia grandiflora*	annual	orange
AUTUMN SAGE	*Salvia greggii*	0	red, hot pink, purple, and white
BAT-FACED CUPHEA	*Cuphea llavea*	28, root hardy to 20	red with dark purple stamens
BLACKFOOT DAISY	*Melampodium luecanthum*	−20	white with yellow eyes
BLUE GRAMA GRASS	*Bouteloua gracilis*	−30	straw-colored seed heads
CALIFORNIA POPPY	*Eschscholtzia californica*	annual	orange

Perennials, Wildflowers, and Grasses (continued)

COMMON NAME	BOTANICAL NAME	COLD HARDINESS (°F)	FLOWER COLOR
CANYON PENSTEMON, DESERT PENSTEMON, MOJAVE BEARDTONGUE	Penstemon pseudospectabilis	5	dark pink
CHERRY SAGE	Salvia microphylla	15	cherry red
CHOCOLATE FLOWER	Berlandiera lyrata	−20	yellow
CLEVELAND SAGE	Salvia clevelandii	10	blue
COOPER'S PAPERFLOWER	Psilostrophe cooperi	10	bright yellow
DAMIANITA DAISY	Chrysactinia mexicana	0	bright yellow
DEER GRASS	Muhlenbergia rigens	0	straw-colored seed heads
DESERT BLUEBELLS	Phacelia campanularia	annual	true blue
DESERT LOBELIA	Lobelia laxiflora	10	red with peach
DESERT LUPINE, COULTER'S LUPINE	Lupinus sparsiflorus	annual	deep blue
DESERT MARIGOLD	Baileya multiradiata	10	bright yellow
DESERT MILKWEED	Asclepias subulata	23	sulfur yellow
DESERT SENNA	Senna covesii	15	yellow-orange
DEVIL'S CLAW	Proboscidea parviflora	annual	purple and white with yellow throat
DOGWEED, GOLDEN DOGWEED	Thymophylla pentachaeta (Dyssodia pentachaeta)	0	bright yellow
EVENING-SCENTED STOCK	Matthiola longipetala bicornis	annual	lavender
FIRECRACKER PENSTEMON, EATON'S PENSTEMON	Penstemon eatoni	−10	bright red
FIREWHEEL, BLANKETFLOWER	Gaillardia pulchella	5	red and yellow

Perennials, Wildflowers, and Grasses (continued)

COMMON NAME	BOTANICAL NAME	COLD HARDINESS (°F)	FLOWER COLOR
GIANT SNAPDRAGON, WILD PINK SNAPDRAGON, PALMER'S PENSTEMON, SCENTED PENSTEMON	Penstemon palmeri	−10	light pink
GLOBEMALLOW, DESERT GLOBEMALLOW	Sphaeralcea ambigua	5	orange most common; red, pink, lavender, and white also available
GOLDEN COLUMBINE	Aquilegia chrysantha	−30	light yellow
GOODDING'S VERBENA	Glandularia gooddingii (Verbena gooddingii)	0	denim blue
GREGG'S MIST FLOWER, BONESET, 'BOOTHILL'	Conoclinium greggii (Eupatorium greggii)	0	light blue
'HOMESTEAD PURPLE' VERBENA	Verbena canadensis 'Homestead Purple'	−5	purple
MEXICAN EVENING PRIMROSE	Oenothera speciosa (O. berlandieri)	0	pink
MEXICAN FEATHER GRASS	Nassella tenuissima (Stipa tenuissima)	0	tawny seed heads
MEXICAN GOLD POPPY	Eschscholtzia mexicana	annual	golden yellow
MEXICAN HAT, CONEFLOWER	Ratibida columnaris	5	bright yellow
MOSS VERBENA, ROCK VERBENA	Glandularia pulchella (Verbena tenuisecta)	20	purple, pink, and white
MT. LEMMON MARIGOLD	Tagetes lemmonii	5	gold
PARRY'S PENSTEMON	Penstemon parryi	15	hot pink
PRAIRIE ZINNIA	Zinnia grandiflora	0	yellow-orange
PRICKLY POPPY	Argemone platyceras	−10	white with yellow centers
ROCK PENSTEMON	Penstemon baccharifolius	5	red
RUSSIAN SAGE	Perovskia atriplicifolia	−20	purple-blue

Perennials, Wildflowers, and Grasses (continued)

COMMON NAME	BOTANICAL NAME	COLD HARDINESS (°F)	FLOWER COLOR
SACRED DATURA	Datura wrightii	5	white
SCARLET MONKEY FLOWER	Mimulus cardinalis	−20	orange-red
SHRUBBY SENNA	Senna wislizenii (Cassia wislizenii)	10	gold
'SIERRA GOLD', GOLDEN DALEA	Dalea capitata 'Sierra Gold'	0	bright yellow
SIERRA SUNDROPS	Calylophus drummondii	5	bright yellow
SONORAN JUSTICIA, SONORAN HONEYSUCKLE	Justicia sonorae	10	purple
SONORAN NIGHTSHADE	Solanum tridynamum	26, root hardy to 20	purple or white
SPREADING FLEABANE	Erigeron divergens	−10	white with yellow centers
SUCCULENT LUPINE, ARROYO LUPINE	Lupinus succulentus	annual	true blue
SUNDROPS, LEMON SUNDROPS	Calylophus hartwegii	5	butter yellow
SUPERB PENSTEMON, CORAL PENSTEMON	Penstemon superbus	5	coral red
TEXAS BETONY	Stachys coccinea	root hardy to 5	red
TEXAS VIOLET SAGE	Salvia farinacea	0	blue with lavender calyxes
TOHOKA DAISY, TAHOKA DAISY, PRAIRIE ASTER	Aster tanacetifolius	0	light purple
TUFTED EVENING PRIMROSE	Oenothera caespitosa	root hardy to −20	white
WHIRLING BUTTERFLIES	Gaura lindheimeri	−10	white or pink
YERBA MANSA	Anemopsis californica	15	zinc-oxide white

VINES

COMMON NAME	BOTANICAL NAME	COLD HARDINESS (°F)	FLOWER COLOR
ARIZONA GRAPE IVY	Cissus trifoliata	15	insignificant flowers
'BAJA RED' QUEEN'S WREATH	Antigonon leptopus 'Baja Red'	20, root hardy to 15	magenta red
"STINKY" PASSION VINE	Passiflora foetida	20, root hardy to 15	light blue
TWINING SNAPDRAGON	Maurandya antirrhiniflora	15	red, purple, or white
YELLOW MORNING GLORY VINE	Merremia aurea	20, root hardy to 15	bright yellow
YELLOW ORCHID VINE	Callaeum macropterum (Mascagnia macroptera)	root hardy to 20	bright yellow

AGAVES, ALOES, CACTI, AND YUCCAS

COMMON NAME	BOTANICAL NAME	COLD HARDINESS (°F)	FLOWER COLOR
ARGENTINE TOOTHPICK, TOOTHPICK CACTUS	Stetsonia coryne	15	white
ARIZONA QUEEN OF THE NIGHT, NIGHT-BLOOMING CEREUS	Peniocereus greggii	5	white
ARTICHOKE AGAVE	Agave parryi var. truncata	20	yellow
BAJA "PUNK ROCK HAIRDO" BARREL CACTUS	Ferocactus rectispinus	22	unknown
BEAKED YUCCA	Yucca rostrata	0	cream
BEAVERTAIL PRICKLY PEAR	Opuntia basilaris	5	magenta
"BIG PINK PINCUSHION"	Mammillaria guelzowiana	26	shocking pink
BISHOP'S CAP	Astrophytum myriostigma	15	yellow with red throats

Agaves, Aloes, Cacti, and Yuccas (continued)

COMMON NAME	BOTANICAL NAME	COLD HARDINESS (°F)	FLOWER COLOR
'BLUE ELF' ALOE	Aloe hybrid 'Blue Elf'	20	orange-red
BLUE YUCCA	Yucca rigida	10	cream
CANDELILLA	Euphorbia antisyphilitica	15	white with pink streaks
CLARET CUP CACTUS	Echinocereus triglochidiatus	10	orange to deep red
DESERT SPOON	Dasylirion wheeleri	0	white
DINNER PLATE PRICKLY PEAR, CLOCKFACE PRICKLY PEAR, ROBUST PRICKLY PEAR	Opuntia robusta	15	yellow
"ELEGANT OAXACAN PINCUSHION"	Mammillaria supertexta	25	pink
ENGELMANN'S PRICKLY PEAR	Opuntia engelmannii	0	pale yellow
FIRE BARREL	Ferocactus pringlei	15	yellow to red
FISHHOOK BARREL	Ferocactus wislizeni	0	yellow-orange
GENTRY'S AGAVE	Agave parryi var. truncata Gentry	15	gold
GOLDEN BARREL	Echinocactus grusonii	15	pale yellow
HEDGEHOG CACTUS	Echinocereus engelmannii	15	magenta
INDIAN FIG PRICKLY PEAR, NOPAL	Opuntia ficus-indica	20	yellow to apricot
'LOS ANGELES' TORCH CACTUS	Echinopsis hybrid 'Los Angeles'	15	pink
MESCAL CENIZA	Agave colorata	14	gold
MEXICAN BLUE BARREL	Ferocactus glaucescens	10	sulfur yellow
MEXICAN FENCEPOST CACTUS	Pachycereus marginatus	28	white
MEXICAN HAIRY BARREL	Ferocactus stainsii	18	yellow to red

Agaves, Aloes, Cacti, and Yuccas (continued)

COMMON NAME	BOTANICAL NAME	COLD HARDINESS (°F)	FLOWER COLOR
MOON CACTUS	Harrisia bonplandii	19	white
NEW MEXICO AGAVE	Agave parryi var. neomexicana (A. neomexicana)	0	gold
OCAHUI AGAVE	Agave ocahui	15	yellow
OCTOPUS AGAVE	Agave vilmoriniana	20	yellow
OWL'S EYES	Mammillaria parkinsonii	20	pink
PALMER'S AGAVE	Agave palmeri	5	chartreuse-yellow
PARRY'S AGAVE	Agave parryi	5	gold
PERUVIAN APPLE CACTUS, HEDGE CACTUS	Cereus hildmannianus (C. peruvianus)	25	white
PONYTAIL PALM	Nolina recurvata	25	no significant bloom
QUEEN VICTORIA AGAVE	Agave victoriae-reginae	15	gold
SAGUARO	Carnegiea gigantea	21	white
SAN PEDRO	Echinopsis pachanoi	25	white
SANTA RITA PRICKLY PEAR, PURPLE PRICKLY PEAR	Opuntia violacea santa-rita	5	yellow
SHARKSKIN AGAVE HYBRID	Agave scabra x ferdinand-regis	15	yellow
SLIPPER PLANT	Pedilanthus macrocarpus	28	red
"SNOW-CAPPED" PINCUSHION	Mammillaria polythele var. nudum	32	magenta
SOFT-TIPPED AGAVE	Agave polyacantha	25	yellow
TORCH CACTUS	Trichocereus hybrid	10	various
TOTEMPOLE CACTUS	Pachycereus schottii var. monstrosus (Lophocereus schottii var. monstrosus)	25	pink

Agaves, Aloes, Cacti, and Yuccas (continued)

COMMON NAME	BOTANICAL NAME	COLD HARDINESS (°F)	FLOWER COLOR
TREE CHOLLA	Cylindropuntia imbricata	5	magenta
TUXEDO SPINE PRICKLY PEAR	Opuntia violacea var. macrocentra	5	bright yellow with orange-red centers
TWIN FLOWERED AGAVE	Agave geminiflora	24	yellow
TWISTED-LEAF YUCCA	Yucca rupicola	0	white
VARIEGATED CENTURY PLANT	Agave americana var. marginata	15	yellow
WEBER'S AGAVE	Agave weberi	10	yellow
WHITE STRIPE AGAVE	Agave americana var. mediopicta	15	yellow
YELLOW HESPERALOE	Hesperaloe parviflora 'Yellow'	12	sulfur yellow

HIGH-ELEVATION TREES

COMMON NAME	BOTANICAL NAME	COLD HARDINESS (°F)	FLOWER COLOR
BIGTOOTH MAPLE	Acer grandidentatum	−30	small, chartreuse
BRISTLECONE PINE	Pinus aristata	−40	red new cones
CURL-LEAF MOUNTAIN MAHOGANY	Cercocarpus ledifolius	−30	insignificant, light yellow
GAMBEL OAK	Quercus gambellii	−30	insignificant
ONE-SEED JUNIPER	Juniperus monosperma	−20	insignificant flowers, blue-green berries
PIÑON PINE	Pinus edulis	−20	insignificant flowers, edible seeds

HIGH-ELEVATION SHRUBS

COMMON NAME	BOTANICAL NAME	COLD HARDINESS (°F)	FLOWER COLOR
APACHE PLUME	*Fallugia paradoxa*	−30	white with showy pink seed heads
BIG SAGEBRUSH	*Artemisia tridentata*	−30	insignificant
CLIFF ROSE	*Purshia mexicana (Cowania mexicana)*	−20	cream
DWARF MUGO PINE	*Pinus mugo mugo*	−30	insignificant
FRINGED SAGE	*Artemisia frigida*	−30	small yellow
RABBITBRUSH, CHAMISA	*Ericameria nauseosa (Chrysothamnus nauseosus)*	−30	shocking gold
SILVER SAGE	*Artemisia ludviciana*	−30	insignificant
THREE LEAF SUMAC, LEMONADE BERRY, SKUNKBUSH	*Rhus trilobata*	−20	not showy, small and chartreuse; red fruit is good in lemonade
TRUE MOUNTAIN MAHOGANY	*Cercocarpus montanus*	−30	cream

HIGH-ELEVATION PERENNIALS, WILDFLOWERS, AND GRASSES

COMMON NAME	BOTANICAL NAME	COLD HARDINESS (°F)	FLOWER COLOR
BLACKFOOT DAISY	*Melampodium luecanthum*	−20	white with yellow eyes
BLUE FESCUE	*Festuca ovina glauca*	−20	tawny brown seed heads
BLUE GRAMA GRASS	*Bouteloua gracilis*	−30	straw-colored seed heads
BLUE OAT GRASS	*Helictotrichon sempervirens*	−20	tawny brown seed heads
BUFFALO GOURD	*Cucurbita foetidissima*	0	cream yellow
CATMINT	*Nepeta x faassenii*	−20	lavender blue

High-Elevation Perennials, Wildflowers, and Grasses (continued)

COMMON NAME	BOTANICAL NAME	COLD HARDINESS (°F)	FLOWER COLOR
CHOCOLATE FLOWER	Berlandiera lyrata	−20	yellow
COLORADO FOUR O'CLOCK, DESERT FOUR O'CLOCK	Mirabilis multiflora	−20	purple-magenta
CORAL BELLS	Heuchera sanguinea	−20	coral pink or bright red
DOUBLE BUBBLE MINT, TEXAS HUMMINGBIRD MINT	Agastache cana	−30	rose-purple
FIRECRACKER PENSTEMON, EATON'S PENSTEMON	Penstemon eatoni	−10	bright red
FIREWHEEL, BLANKETFLOWER	Gaillardia pulchella	5	red and yellow
GIANT SNAPDRAGON, WILD PINK SNAPDRAGON, PALMER'S PENSTEMON, SCENTED PENSTEMON	Penstemon palmeri	−10	light pink
GOLDEN COLUMBINE	Aquilegia chrysantha	−30	light yellow
'HOMESTEAD PURPLE' VERBENA	Verbena canadensis 'Homestead Purple'	−5	purple
LICORICE MINT, SUNSET HYSSOP	Agastache rupestris	−10	pink and orange
MAT PENSTEMON	Penstemon caespitosus	−20	lavender purple
MEXICAN EVENING PRIMROSE	Oenothera speciosa (O. berlandieri)	0	pink
MEXICAN FEATHER GRASS	Stipa tenuissima (Nassella tenuissima)	0	tawny seed heads
MISSOURI EVENING PRIMROSE	Oenothera missourensis	−20	lemon yellow
PITCHER'S SAGE	Salvia azurea grandiflora (S. pitcheri)	−20	azure blue
PRICKLY POPPY	Argemone platyceras	−10	white with yellow centers
ROCKY MOUNTAIN IRIS	Iris missourensis	−20	blue and white
ROCKY MOUNTAIN PENSTEMON	Penstemon strictus	−30	midnight blue

High-Elevation Perennials, Wildflowers, and Grasses (continued)

COMMON NAME	BOTANICAL NAME	COLD HARDINESS (°F)	FLOWER COLOR
RUSSIAN SAGE	*Perovskia atriplicifolia*	–20	purple-blue
SCARLET MONKEY FLOWER	*Mimulus cardinalis*	–20	orange-red
SCARLET PENSTEMON, BEARDLIP PENSTEMON	*Penstemon barbatus*	–20	red
SPREADING FLEABANE	*Erigeron divergens*	–10	white with yellow centers
TOHOKA DAISY, TAHOKA DAISY, PRAIRIE ASTER	*Aster tanacetifolius*	0	light purple
TUFTED EVENING PRIMROSE	*Oenothera caespitosa*	root hardy to –20	white
UPRIGHT VERBENA	*Verbena bonariensis*	13, annual in cold climates	purple
UTAH STATE UNIVERSITY PENSTEMON	*Penstemon 'U.S.U.'*	–10	purplish-pink
WHIRLING BUTTERFLIES	*Gaura lindheimeri*	–10	white or pink

HIGH-ELEVATION AGAVES, CACTI, AND YUCCAS

COMMON NAME	BOTANICAL NAME	COLD HARDINESS (°F)	FLOWER COLOR
BEAKED YUCCA	*Yucca rostrata*	0	cream
BEAVERTAIL PRICKLY PEAR	*Opuntia basilaris*	5	magenta
DESERT SPOON	*Dasylirion wheeleri*	0	white
ENGELMANN'S PRICKLY PEAR	*Opuntia engelmannii*	0	pale yellow
FISHHOOK BARREL	*Ferocactus wislizeni*	0	yellow-orange
NEW MEXICO AGAVE	*Agave parryi var. neomexicana (A. neomexicana)*	0	gold
TWISTED-LEAF YUCCA	*Yucca rupicola*	0	white

appendix C:
FAQ about rainwater cisterns

In what situations do culvert-type cisterns work best?

Cisterns are great in small spaces that would make creating swales impractical. They also are effective in very heavy soils where swales would create standing water for long periods of time. Cisterns allow rainwater to be stored for longer periods of time. They also allow the water to be applied to plants at a slower rate via a drip system or other means. Small gardens are usually ideal candidates for cisterns.

Can I hook up a drip system to a cistern?

Yes. A drip system will run off of the pressure in the cistern, but it needs to be designed for low pressure. Depending on their height, most cisterns produce less than 10 psi. Experience has shown that Rainbird two-gallon-per-hour irrigation emitters or four-gallon-per-hour flag-type emitters work best.

How much rainfall can I collect?

This depends on when the rain comes. In general, during southern Arizona's two rainy seasons, your cisterns will overflow. It is usually impractical to install enough large cisterns to capture every drop. Your roof will almost always shed much more water than you can collect. The formula for figuring out how many gallons of water your roof will generate is the roof catchment area (square feet) times the average yearly rainfall (inches) times 550 gallons, divided by 1,000. If you can capture half of this runoff, you will be doing well.

How can I camouflage my cistern?

The cisterns we use are upended galvanized culverts. Most folks either love them or hate them. They can be painted. The most elegant way to hide your cistern is to put a trellis around it and grow vines.

How do I know how much water is in my cistern?

Besides going out in the rain in your underwear and climbing up a ladder to look inside, you can rig up a simple gauge on the side of your cistern.

Will I get mosquitoes inside my tank?

If you keep the tank covered with a floating lid (Styrofoam) you should not have mosquito problems. You can also use BT tablets, which will kill any mosquito larvae that manage to make it into the tank.

appendix D:
where to buy, see, and learn about desert plants

Purveyors of Fine Southwestern Plants and Garden Tools

Arizona

B & B Cactus Farm

11550 East Speedway Boulevard, Tucson, 85748

520-721-4687

Owned and operated by former Arizona-Sonora Desert Museum horticulturist and cactus guru Mark Sitter, this is the premier large-specimen cactus nursery in Tucson. Great service and information without a big corporate-nursery feel.

Bach's Greenhouse Cactus Nursery

8602 North Thornydale Road, Tucson, 85742

520-744-3333, www.bachs-cacti.com

Huge cactus and succulent selection, with a fine demonstration garden featuring really big specimens.

Baker Nursery

3414 North 40th Street, Phoenix, 85018

602-955-4500

A Phoenix institution with a nice mix of native and traditional landscape plants.

Civano Nursery

5301 South Houghton Road, Tucson, 85747

520-546-9200, www.civanonursery.com

Specializing in Sonoran, Chihuahuan, and Mohave Desert native plants, Civano Nursery retails a wide selection of woody and herbaceous plants, many of them grown at its state-of-the-art 70-acre farm. One of the largest native-plant nurseries in Arizona.

Desert Survivors Native Plant Nursery

1020 West Starr Pass Boulevard, Tucson, 85713

520-361-3071, www.desertsurvivors.org/nursery.asp

A nursery that is also a charitable organization with a twice-annual sale on native plants.

Flagstaff Native Plant and Seed

400 East Butler Avenue, Flagstaff, 86001

928-773-9406, www.nativeplantandseed.com

This cozy little nursery in the pines has a fine selection of just what it sounds like: native plants and seeds. A great source for hard-to-find items from catchfly to sideoats grama seed.

Greenfire Books

925 East Fort Lowell Road, Tucson, 85719

520-408-0677, www.greenfirebooks.com

Greenfire gets its name from an Aldo Leopold quote and specializes in books about the plants, animals, people, and environment of the desert Southwest.

Landscape Cacti

7711 West Bopp Road, Tucson, 85735

520-883-0200

Owner and cactus doctor Jon Weeks is passionate about cacti. He carefully selects his specimens for form and coloration. Impeccably clean cacti, hardened off for the sun and the cold in a rural Tucson location.

Mountain States Wholesale Nursery

Glendale, www.mswn.com

The granddaddy of native plant nurseries, MSWN has been a Xeriscape tastemaker since 1963. A wholesale-only nursery; website contains a wealth of information for consumers, including where to buy the plants they grow. A staff of top-notch horticulturists keeps MSWN pushing the envelope.

Native Seeds/SEARCH

526 North 4th Avenue, Tucson, 85705

520-622-5561, www.nativeseeds.org

This great outfit promotes both crop biodiversity and cultural diversity through its seed bank and outreach programs that help Native Americans rediscover wild foods. More types of native beans, chiles, and corn than you can shake a stick at.

Plants for the Southwest

50 East Blacklidge Drive, Tucson, 85705

520-628-8773, www.lithops.com

A charming little nursery tucked away right in the middle of town. Lots of succulents, cacti, and unique pottery. Great service and a fine selection of lithops or "living stones" (low-growing succulents from Africa that look like small pebbles or babies' toes).

Shady Way Gardens

566 West Superstition Boulevard, Apache Junction, 85220

480-288-9655

Tiny nursery with unusual native plants like white Parry's penstemon.

Southwest Gardener

2809 North 15th Avenue, Phoenix, 85007

602-0279-9510, www.southwestgardener.com

Conveniently located near downtown, with one of the best selections of quirky garden art, tools, and garden books around, plus anything from French garden furniture to hard-to-find seeds. Great class series and newsletter. If they don't have it, they will order it.

Spadefoot Nursery

8897 East Walnut Trail, Pearce, 85625

520-824-3247

Specializing in native oaks, this little nursery is a southeastern Arizona gem. Owned and run by Petey Mesquitey, a native-plant radio celebrity. Open by appointment only.

Starr Nursery

3340 West Ruthann Road, Tucson, 85745

520-743-7052

Agave master and plant explorer Greg Starr runs the show here, by appointment only.

Wild Seed

6615 South 28th Street, Phoenix, 85285

602-276-3536

One of the first sources, and still the best, for desert wildflower seeds. Owner Rita Jo Anthony is both charming and expert in explaining the mysteries of seeds.

California

Las Pilitas Nursery

8331 Nelson Way, Escondido, 92026

760-749-5930, www.laspilitas.com

A funky little nursery under some nice sycamores that has loads of cool southern California natives, like the *Salvia apiana* I purchased on a recent trip.

Tree of Life Nursery/Round House Plant Store

33201 Ortega Highway, San Juan Capistrano, 92693

949-728-0685, www.treeoflifenursery.com

The largest supplier of native plants in the state. A truly awesome printed catalog with over 500 species and varieties, complete with planting guides (and a photo of a tractor-riding farmer surfing). Head honchos Mike Evans and Jeff Bohn put a lot a fun and passion into their business. Their retail side, Round House Plant Store, sells plants and books to the public.

Yerba Buena Native Plant Nursery
19500 Skyline Boulevard, Woodside, 94062
650-851-1668, www.yerbabuenanursery.com
California's oldest retail native-plant nursery, growing over 600 native varieties. Garden shop with pastries on weekends and even high tea on several dates each year. The most civilized native-plant purveyor in California.

Colorado

Sunscapes Rare Plant Nursery
330 Carlile Avenue, Pueblo, 80521
719-546-0047, www.sunscapes.net
Their online catalog is as interesting as it is diverse. A great place to shop if you want to find xeric plants that have not found their way in to the garden centers.

New Mexico

Agua Fria Nursery
1409 Agua Fria Road, Santa Fe, 87505
505-983-4831
A great little family-owned nursery.

Agua Viva Seed Ranch
Route 1, Box 8, Taos, 87571
505-758-4520
A fine source for wild seed in New Mexico.

Bernardo Beach Native Plant Farm
3729 Arno Street NE, Albuquerque, 87107
505-345-6248
Respected author Judith Phillips owns this wholesale and retail nursery.

Enchanted Gardens
413 West Griggs Avenue, Las Cruces, 88005
505-524-1886, www.nmenchantedgardens.com
With plants from Texas tuberose to desert zinnia, this is a fine little nursery in Las Cruces.

Helen's Native Plants
10147 2nd NW, Albuquerque, 87114
505-898-5227
Plants, wholesale and retail sales.

Plants of the Southwest
3095 Agua Fria Road, Santa Fe, 87507
505-438-8888,
and 6680 Fourth Street NW, Albuquerque, 87107
505-344-8830, www.plantsofthesouthwest.com
A great New Mexico source for wild plants and info. Lots of hard-to-find plants, with retail locations in both Santa Fe and Albuquerque; great mail-order service.

Rowlands Nursery
7404 Menaul Boulevard NE, Albuquerque, 87110
505-883-5727,
540 Telshor Boulevard, Las Cruces, 88001
505-522-4227, www.erowlands.com
The oldest and largest independent nursery in New Mexico.

Santa Fe Greenhouses, DBA High Country Gardens
2902 Rufina Street, Santa Fe, 87507
800-925-9387, www.highcountrygardens.com
Simply the best source for high-elevation Xeriscape plants on the planet, with superb printed and online catalogs. They mail-order everywhere. Many of the plants in our award-winning Great Basin garden came from here. If you visit, don't miss the fabulous demonstration garden near the parking lot.

Seed of Change
P.O. Box 15700, Santa Fe, 87506
505-438-8080, 888-762-7333 for catalog,
www.seedsofchange.com
A fine selection of open-pollinated, organically grown seeds.

Sierra Vista Growers
2800 NM Highway 28, La Union, 88027
505-874-2415
Good selection of New Mexico natives.

Texas

Kimas Tejas Nursery
962 State Highway 71E, Bastrop, 78602
512-303-4769, www.texasgrown.com
You can't help but love a nursery that has its own
theme song, recorded at the Chicken Shack in south
Austin. You can hear it on their website—really. They
also carry a full line of natives and organic gardening
products.

Native American Seed
127 North 16th, Junction, 76849
800-728-4043, www.seedsource.com
Bill and Jan Neiman run a mail-order and retail
seed store that, in their own words, "goes beyond
bluebonnets." If you want to know what kind of grass
your buffalo will like, ask here.

Natives of Texas: Hill Country Native Plants
4256 Medina Highway, Kerrville, 78028
830-896-2169, www.nativesoftexas.com
Oaks, oaks, oaks, and madrones, plus many other fine
local plants.

Native Texas Nursery
16019 Milo Road, Austin, 78725
512-276-9801
I have it on good information that some of the native
plants in Laura Bush's Crawford, Texas, garden came
from this fine wholesale nursery.

One Way Nursery
308 West Avenue E, Alpine, 79830
432-837-1117
A great little nursery full of west Texas plants.

Rainbow Gardens
8516 Bandera Road, San Antonio, 78250
210-680-2394, www.rainbowgardens.biz
Helping San Antonians save water with a broad
selection of Xeriscape plants.

Sweetbriar Nursery
13999 FM 2305, Belton, 76513
254-780-4233, www.vvm.com/~reid
If you can't find it anywhere else in Texas, you may
want to check with Reid Lewis at Sweetbriar. Rare and
hard-to-find natives are his stock and trade.

Wildseed Farms
425 Wildflower Hills, Fredericksburg, 78624
800-848-0078, www.wildseedfarms.com
The largest wildflower seed grower in Texas.

Yucca Do Nursery
FM 35 and FM 3346, Hempstead, 77445
979-826-4580, www.yuccado.com
A great nursery between Houston and Austin carrying
many rare plants from the Texas-Mexico border region.
Adjacent to the entertainingly named Peckerwood
Garden (www.peckerwoodgarden.com), also open to
the public.

Utah

Great Basin Natives
310 South Main, Holden, 84636
gbn@greatbasinnatives.com,
www.greatbasinnatives.com
This family nursery in the tiny town of Holden,
population 500, is a great source for Great Basin
plants. Because of their high, cold location, you can be
sure what they sell is cold-hardy. They do ship mail-
order; contact them via e-mail or regular mail to order.

High Desert Gardens
2971 South Highway 191, Moab, 84532-3438
435-259-4531
A good place for the people of red rocks country to
buy penstemons and other desert plants once absent
from the Republic of Moab retail outlets.

Lone Peak Conservation Nursery

271 West Bitterbrush Lane, Draper, 84020-8670
801-571-0900,
www.ffsl.utah.gov/lonepeak/nursery/LPNursery.htm
This state-owned facility, which serves as a work
program for prison inmates, grows over 80 varieties of
Great Basin native woody shrubs and trees. They sell
only seedlings, and the minimum order is 100. As I
mentioned in the chapter on my Utah garden, in the
early 1990s this was one of the few places to find
native plants in Utah.

Wildland Nursery

370 East 600 North, Joseph, 84739
435-527-1234, www.wildlandnursery.com
It figures that at about the same time we left Utah, the
countryside began to be dotted with native-plant
growers. I haven't been here, but they have a good
website and a good plant list.

Willard Bay Gardens

7095 South Highway 89, Willard, 84340
435-723-1834 or 801-782-8984
The best selection of drought-tolerant perennials in
Utah. Expert, friendly service. Run by the husband
and wife team of Della and Barney Barnett,
horticulturists extraordinaire.

Gardens to Visit

*Most of these gardens have annual plant sales, and some
have year-round nurseries. These plant sales and nurseries
are often the best sources for hard-to-find native plants.*

Arizona

The Arboretum at Flagstaff

4001 Woody Mountain Road, Flagstaff, 86001
928-774-1442, www.thearb.org

More than just hippies driving bio-diesel tractors,
Flagstaff Arboretum is a high-elevation native-plant
lover's paradise. The meadows and mass plantings
provide good cool summer fun.

Arizona-Sonora Desert Museum

2021 North Kinney Road, Tucson, 85743
520-883-1380, www.desertmuseum.org
Part botanical garden, part zoo, this world-class
institution is one of the most-visited destinations in
the Southwest. Some of the most intricate desert
gardens anywhere. Not to be missed.

Boyce Thompson Arboretum

37615 U.S. Highway 60, Superior, 85273
520-689-2723, http://arboretum.ag.arizona.edu
Tucked away in a canyon northeast of Phoenix, Boyce
Thompson has a collection of 3,200 species of plants,
800 of which are cacti. Its many themed gardens,
including the desert legume garden, make it well
worth the trip.

Desert Botanical Garden

1201 North Galvin Parkway, Phoenix, 85008
480-941-1225, www.dbg.org
Spectacular rainwater harvesting using a giant sunken
spiral as well as a world-famous cactus collection,
wildflower trail, and butterfly pavilion. The DBG also
offers some of the best garden-design and landscape
courses in the arid West.

Steele Indian School Park

300 East Indian School Road, Phoenix, 85012
602-495-0739, http://phoenix.gov/PARKS/sisp.html
For desert plant enthusiasts, the Christy Ten-Eyck-
designed 15-acre entry garden may be the best reason
to visit this free public park downtown. The design's
circular pathway spirals downward through terraced
displays of native plants, with Native American poems
etched into the concrete. At the bottom lies a giant
concrete water feature surrounded by cottonwood trees.

Tohono Chul Park

7366 North Paseo del Norte, Tucson, 85704

520-742-6455, www.tohonochulpark.org

With its new greenhouse and Sin Agua Garden, Tohono Chul keeps getting better and better each year. A desert rat's paradise, featuring some of the best demonstration gardens in the arid West. Excellent selection of hard-to-find native plants.

Tucson Botanical Gardens

2150 North Alvernon Way, Tucson, 85712

520-326-9686, www.tucsonbotanical.org

Nice mix of xeric and traditional gardens. My favorites include an eclectic barrio garden with Spanish signage and a Tohono O'odham traditional garden with waffle-shaped planting beds.

University of Arizona Campus Arboretum

U of A Campus, Tucson, 85721

520-884-7516, http://arboretum.arizona.edu

This newly designated arboretum, much of which is the work of distinguished horticulturist Warren Jones, is home to some of the largest tree specimens in the state as well as the Joseph Wood Krutch Cactus Garden, named after the respected nature writer.

California

The Huntington Library, Art Collections, and Botanical Gardens

1151 Oxford Road, San Marino, 91108

626-405-2100, www.huntington.org

A collection of cacti so vast you could wander half the day. Includes mass plantings of golden barrel cacti, artichoke agaves, and other succulents from both hemispheres. A must-see for succulent lovers.

The Living Desert Zoo and Gardens

47-900 Portola Avenue, Palm Desert, 92260

760-346-5694, www.livingdesert.org

This California zoo and desert gardens may be the best place to get ideas for a yard in inland southern California. A fine collection of cold-hardy desert plants for California's most inhospitable regions.

Quail Botanical Gardens

230 Quail Gardens Drive, Encinitas, 92024

760-436-3036, www.qbgardens.com

If you want to see what San Diego and L.A. looked like before we planted way too much exotic crap there, then visit Quail. You might fall in love with a few California native plants. A hike through the chaparral garden will get you excited about the diversity of native xeric plants in chaparral-scrub country.

Santa Barbara Botanic Garden

1212 Mission Canyon Road, Santa Barbara, 93105

805-682-4726, www.sbbg.org

In a canyon above the Santa Barbara Mission, this garden's narrow meadows turn into rivers of orange California poppies in the spring. Need I say more?

Colorado

Denver Botanic Gardens

8500 Deer Creek Canyon Road, Denver, 80128

720-865-3500, www.botanicgardens.org

World-famous alpine gardens and stunning penstemon plantings make the Denver Botanical Gardens a destination for high-elevation plant lovers from around the world.

Western Colorado Botanical Gardens

655 Struthers, Grand Junction, 81501

970-245-9030, www.wcbotanic.org

Near Moab, Utah, seasonal xeric garden and Colorado native garden show off some of the great native plants of western Colorado and the Book Cliffs area.

Nevada

Ethel M Botanical Cactus Garden
2 Cactus Garden Drive, Henderson, 89014
702-435-2655, www.ethelm.com
Ethel M Chocolate's breathtaking botanical garden surrounding the chocolate factory is one of the largest collections of its kind. The free chocolate samples (with a factory tour) are also a plus. Four acres of drought-tolerant ornamentals, cacti, and other succulents. A model for desert manufacturers, the factory uses all of its wastewater—32,000 gallons a day—to water its extensive gardens. Did I mention the free chocolate samples?

UNLV Arboretum
University of Nevada–Las Vegas, 4505 Maryland Parkway, Las Vegas, 89154
702-895-3392,
www.unlv.edu/facilities/landscape/arboretum.html
This arboretum includes the entire 335-acre university campus and a two-acre xeric garden (found near the entrance to the Barrick Museum of Natural History).

New Mexico

Rio Grande Botanical Gardens
903 10th Street SW, Albuquerque, 87104
505-764-6200, www.cabq.gov/biopark/garden/
Situated alongside its namesake, the 20-acre botanical garden sits in the middle of the largest cottonwood gallery forest in the world and will give you plenty of good high-elevation planting ideas.

Santa Fe Botanical Garden
P.O. Box 23343, Santa Fe, 87502
505-428-1684
Periodic plant sales.

Texas

Chihuahuan Desert Gardens, UTEP
Centennial Museum (corner of University and Wiggins)
University of Texas–El Paso, El Paso, 79968
915-747-5565,
http://nasa.utep.edu/chih/gardens/gardens.htm
This garden is full of great hardscape ideas (including many walls and pathways constructed of native stone) as well as a fine collection of plants from America's largest desert.

Chihuahuan Desert Research Institute
4 miles south of Fort Davis on Highway 118, Fort Davis, 79734
432-364-2499, www.cdri.org
World's largest collection of Chihuahuan Desert cacti.

Lady Bird Johnson Wildflower Center
4801 La Crosse Avenue, Austin, 78729
512-292-4100, www.wildflower.org
The premier institution for wildflower conservation in the United States. First-rate gardens, symposiums, and classes.

San Antonio Botanical Garden
555 Funston, San Antonio, 78209
210-207-3250, www.sabot.org
The native areas of the garden highlight three regional themes of Texas: Hill Country, the Piney Woods, and the southwest Texas desert. All of the themed gardens include authentic structures like adobe buildings that give the gardens a sense of place.

Utah

Red Butte Garden
300 Wakara Way, Salt Lake City, 84108
801-581-4747
Through its newly expanded low-water-use sections, Red Butte gives living proof that you can create Utah gardens without bluegrass lawns, featuring many plants that define the Great Basin. The spectacular children's garden includes a giant vine-covered "rattlesnake" and a rock grotto.

Southwestern States Native Plant Societies

Arizona Native Plant Society (Tucson)
www.aznps.org
California Botanical Society (Berkeley)
www.calbotsoc.org
California Native Plant Society (Sacramento)
www.cnps.org
Colorado Native Plant Society (Fort Collins)
www.conps.org
Lady Bird Johnson Wildflower Center (Austin, Texas)
www.wildflower.org
Native Plant Society of New Mexico (Las Cruces)
http://npsnm.unm.edu
Native Plant Society of Texas (Georgetown)
www.npsot.org
Southern California Botanists (Fullerton)
www.socalbot.org
Tucson Cactus and Succulent Society (Tucson)
www.tucsoncactus.org
Utah Native Plant Society (Salt Lake City)
www.unps.org

suggested reading

Abbey, Edward. *Cactus Country.* New York: Time-Life Books, 1973.

Anderson, Edward F. *The Cactus Family.* Portland, Oregon: Timber Press, 2001.

Berger, Bruce. *The Telling Distance: Conversations with the American Desert.* Tucson, Arizona: University of Arizona Press, 1997.

Bowers, Janice Emily. *A Full Life in a Small Place and Other Essays from a Desert Garden.* Tucson, Arizona: University of Arizona Press, 1993.

Broyles, Bill. *Our Sonoran Desert.* Tucson, Arizona: Rio Nuevo Publishers, 2003.

Conran, Terence, and Dan Pearson. *The Essential Garden Book.* New York: Three Rivers Press, 1998.

Darke, Rick. *The American Woodland Garden: Capturing the Spirit of the Deciduous Forest.* Portland, Oregon: Timber Press, 2002.

Druse, Ken. *The Natural Habitat Garden.* Portland, Oregon: Timber Press, 1994.

Elliot, Charles. *The Gap in the Hedge: Dispatches from the Extraordinary World of British Gardening.* New York: Lyons Press, 1998.

Epple, Anne Orth. *A Field Guide to the Plants of Arizona.* Helena, Montana: Falcon Publishing, 1995.

Felger, Richard Stephen, Matthew Brian Johnson, and Michael Francis Wilson. *The Trees of Sonora, Mexico.* New York: Oxford University Press, 2001.

Glennon, Robert. *Water Follies: Groundwater Pumping and the Fate of America's Fresh Waters.* Washington, D.C.: Island Press, 2002.

Humphreys, Anna, and Susan Lowell. *Saguaro: The Desert Giant.* Tucson, Arizona: Rio Nuevo Publishers, 2002.

Irish, Gary, and Mary F. Irish. *Agaves, Yuccas, and Related Plants: A Gardener's Guide.* Portland, Oregon: Timber Press, 2000.

Irish, Mary. *Arizona Gardener's Guide.* Nashville, Tennessee: Cool Springs Press, 2002.

—. *Gardening in the Desert: A Guide to Plant Selection and Care.* Tucson, Arizona: University of Arizona Press, 2000.

Jarman, Derek. *Derek Jarman's Garden.* New York: Overlook Press, 1996.

Jones, Warren, and Charles Sacamano. *Landscape Plants for Dry Regions.* New York: Da Capo Press, 2000.

Klinkenborg, Verlyn. *The Rural Life.* Boston, Massachusetts: Little, Brown and Company, 2003.

Knopf, Jim. *The Xeriscape Flower Gardener: A Waterwise Guide for the Rocky Mountain Region.* Boulder, Colorado: Johnson Books, 1991.

McNamee, Gregory. *Gila: The Life and Death of an American River.* Albuquerque, New Mexico: University of New Mexico Press, 1998.

Mielke, Judy. *Native Plants for Southwest Landscapes.* Austin, Texas: University of Texas Press, 1993.

Mitchell, Henry. *The Essential Earthman.* Boston, Massachusetts: Houghton Mifflin Company, 1981.

—. *Henry Mitchell on Gardening.* Boston, Massachusetts: Houghton Mifflin Company, 1998.

Nabhan, Gary Paul. *Coming Home to Eat: The Pleasures and Politics of Local Foods.* New York: W. W. Norton and Company, 2002.

—. *Gathering the Desert.* Tucson, Arizona: University of Arizona Press, 1985.

Nelson, Kim. *A Desert Gardener's Companion.* Tucson, Arizona: Rio Nuevo Publishers, 2001.

Niethammer, Carolyn. *The Prickly Pear Cookbook.* Tucson, Arizona: Rio Nuevo Publishers, 2004.

Peace, Tom. *Sunbelt Gardening: Success in Hot-Weather Climates.* Golden, Colorado: Fulcrum Publishing, 2000.

Phillips, Judith. *Natural by Design: Beauty and Balance in Southwest Gardens.* Santa Fe, New Mexico: Museum of New Mexico Press, 1995.

—. *Plants for Natural Gardens: Southwestern Native and Adaptive Trees, Shrubs, Wildflowers, and Grasses.* Santa Fe, New Mexico: Museum of New Mexico Press, 1995.

Phillips, Steven J., and Patricia Wentworth Comus, eds. *A Natural History of the Sonoran Desert.* Tucson, Arizona, and Berkeley, California: Arizona-Sonora Desert Museum Press and University of California Press, 2000.

Pollan, Michael. *The Botany of Desire: A Plant's Eye View of the World.* New York: Random House, 2001.

—. *A Place of My Own: The Education of an Amateur Builder.* New York: Random House, 1997.

—. *Second Nature: A Gardener's Education.* New York: Delta, 1992.

Quinn, Meg. *Cacti of the Desert Southwest.* Tucson, Arizona: Rio Nuevo Publishers, 2001.

—. *Wildflowers of the Mountain Southwest.* Tucson, Arizona: Rio Nuevo Publishers, 2003.

—. *Wildflowers of the Desert Southwest.* Tucson, Arizona: Rio Nuevo Publishers, 2000.

Springer, Lauren. *The Undaunted Garden: Planting for Weather-Resilient Beauty.* Golden, Colorado: Fulcrum Publishing, 1994.

Turner, Raymond M., Janice Emily Bowers, and Tony L. Burgess. *Sonoran Desert Plants: An Ecological Atlas.* Tucson, Arizona: University of Arizona Press, 1995.

Wasowski, Andy, and Sally Wasowski. *The Landscaping Revolution: Garden with Mother Nature, Not against Her.* Chicago, Illinois: Contemporary Books, 2000.

Wasowski, Sally. *Native Landscaping from El Paso to L.A.* Chicago, Illinois: McGraw-Hill/ Contemporary Books, 2000.

West, Steve. *Northern Chihuahuan Desert Wildflowers: A Field Guide to Wildflowers and Other Plants of the Desert and Its Parklands.* Helena, Montana: Falcon Publishing, 2000.

Wheeler, David. *By Pen and by Spade: An Anthology of Garden Writing from Hortus.* New York: Summit Books, 1990.

Williams, Terry Tempest. *Coyote's Canyon.* Salt Lake City, Utah: Gibbs Smith Books, 1989.

—. *Red: Passion and Patience in the Desert.* New York: Pantheon Books, 2001.

—. *Refuge: An Unnatural History of Family and Place.* New York: Vintage Books, 1992.

index